CULTURES OF THE WORLD®

SAINT LUCIA

Tamra Orr

Marshall Cavendish
Benchmark
New York

PICTURE CREDITS
Cover photo: © Randall Bishop
age fotostock/Blaine Harrington: 79 • age fotostock/Bruno Morandi: 50 • age fotostock/Sylvain Grandadam: 52, 69 • age fotostock/Walter Bibikow: 11 • age fotostock/Yadid Levy: 47 • alt.TYPE/reuters: 40, 108, 109, 110, 111, 112 • Art Director's & Trip: 74, 81, 116 • Audrius Tomonis: 135 • Corbis: 6, 8, 9, 14, 15, 28, 37, 38, 43, 46, 48, 56, 57, 58, 59, 60, 63, 65, 66, 70, 71, 72, 77, 78, 80, 87, 88, 93, 97, 98, 99, 100. 119, 120, 121, 122, 123, 126 • E.Blauer/Laure: 17, 62, 89, 128 • Eye Ubiquitous/Hutchison: 92, 118 • Jason Laure: 13, 36, 55, 84, 94, 95 • Joel Sartore/National Geographic Image Collection: 12, 19, 25, 51, 90, 124, 125 • Masterfile/George Contorakes: 107 • MCIA/Thomas Khoo: 130 • Photolibrary: 1, 3, 4, 5, 7, 18, 20, 22, 23, 24, 26, 32, 35, 44, 45, 67, 68, 85, 86, 96, 104, 105, 106, 113, 117, 127 • Richard Elliot: 76 • Stockfood/Brauner, Michael: 131 • Wides & Holl: 129

PRECEDING PAGE
Young elementary school girls from Anse La Raye in Saint Lucia.

Publisher (U.S.): Michelle Bisson
Editors: Christine Florie, Stephanie Pee, Rizza Manois
Copyreader: Mindy Hicks
Designer: Benson Tan
Cover picture researcher: Connie Gardner
Picture researchers: Thomas Khoo, Joshua Ang

Marshall Cavendish Benchmark
99 White Plains Road
Tarrytown, NY 10591
Web site: www.marshallcavendish.us

Originated and designed by Times Media Private Limited
An imprint of Marshall Cavendish International (Asia) Private Limited
A member of Times Publishing Limited

Library of Congress Cataloging-in-Publication Data
Orr, Tamra.
 Saint Lucia / by Tamra Orr
 p.cm. — (Cultures of the world)
 Summary: "Provides comprehensive information on the geography, history, governmental structure, economy, cultural diversity, peoples, religion, and culture of Saint Lucia"—Provided by publisher.
 Includes bibliographical references and index.
 ISBN 978-0-7614-2569-4
1.Saint Lucia—Juvenile literature. I. Title. II. Title: Saint Lucia. III. Series.

F2100.O77 2008
972.9843—dc22   2006038625

Printed in China
7 6 5 4 3 2 1

CONTENTS

A man selling fresh produce in Saint Lucia.

The waters of Saint Lucia teem with marine life such as this hawksbill turtle.

INTRODUCTION

ONE OF THE LARGEST ISLANDS IN the Windward Island group, Saint Lucia (Saint LOO-sha) looks like it popped right out of a book about paradise. It has lush green trees, bright black and gold sandy beaches, and a huge variety of colorful plants and flowers. From its mountains to its rain forests, Saint Lucia is a place that invites people to stop by and stay for a while—or forever.

Saint Lucia was fiercely fought over by several European countries. Its location was perfect for pirates to hide out and strategically right for both France and England to use for settlements and plantations. The island actually changed hands 14 times and earned the title "Helen of the West Indies" in reference to Helen of Troy, one of the most sought after women in Greek history.

Home to more than 168,000 people, Saint Lucia struggles with high rates of unemployment and poverty. However, despite its problems, Saint Lucia truly lives up to its motto, "The Land, The People, The Light."

GEOGRAPHY

THERE IS AN OLD saying that states "good things come in small packages." Nowhere is this truer than in Saint Lucia. Although it is one of the largest of the Windward Island group, it is still only 236 square miles (515 sq km), or just slightly larger than the size of Chicago, Illinois. An experienced bike rider could certainly tour the whole island in a day, since Saint Lucia is 27 miles (43 km) long and 14 miles (22 km) wide.

Saint Lucia can be found among the chain of islands that make up the West Indies. Like a string of pearls, these islands wrap around the eastern end of the Caribbean Sea on the western side with the Atlantic Ocean. The West Indies are made up of the Bahamas and the Greater and Lesser Antilles. Farther toward South America are the Lesser Antilles. This area is further broken down into the Windward Islands to the south and the Leeward Islands to the north. Why do they have these names? It is because they are exposed to the blowing of the northwest trade winds.

The Windward Islands include Dominica, Grenada, Saint Vincent and the Grenadines, Martinique, and Saint Lucia. Saint Lucia's closest ocean neighbors are Martinique at 21 miles (33 km) to the north and Barbados 90–100 miles (144–160 km) to the southeast. Florida is about 1,300 miles (2,092 km) away.

Above: **Saint Lucia is part of the Windward Islands.**

Opposite: **The twin peaks of Saint Lucia, Gros Piton and Petit Piton, are known for their emerald green forested slopes.**

7

A LAND OF DIVERSITY

Unlike its neighbor the Bahamas, Saint Lucia is not made up of coral and sand. Instead it was created by volcanic rock. There are places in the southwest region of North America that mirror the island's beginnings. In Saint Lucia boiling and bubbling pools of mud fill the air with the smell of sulfur and other gases.

Although it is not an island full of mountain ranges, Saint Lucia is far from flat. Its tallest point is Mount Gimie, a 3,117 foot (950 m) peak. The island also has the "twin peaks," as they are known. Gros Piton and Petit Piton ("large" and "little mountain peaks" in French) rise out of the sea to almost 3,000 feet (914 m) each. At first they look like they

Bubbling pools of mud are found in volcanic sulphur springs around Saint Lucia.

Saint Lucia boasts dense
rain forests protected by
the UNESCO.

are one mountain, but upon closer inspection it becomes evident that they are separate. Their emerald green forested slopes are often the first thing that visitors see as they approach the island. Although many are tempted to scale the sides of these volcanic giants, it is a dangerous trek for the inexperienced climber. Landslides are common, and trails are rugged and hazardous. The two peaks cannot be climbed without government permission.

The center of Saint Lucia has the highest mountains. Rising 1,000 feet (304 km) above sea level, this area is covered in heavy vegetation and rain forests. Waterfalls send gallons of water cascading and roaring down to the streams and rivers waiting below. Multiple rivers are created and flow from the central region, back out to the surrounding sea.

The rain forests cover 19,000 acres (7,689 ha) and are protected by the United Nations Educational, Scientific and Cultural Organization (UNESCO) as a natural world heritage site. The interior of the island is also where the most fertile valleys are found. Banana plantations are located there to take advantage of the vast quantities of moist soil and sunshine.

The northern part of the island is the least populated. Here it is much drier, and there is more scrubland covered in cacti and century plants. It often takes more than 10 years for one to bloom. When it is getting ready, it grows quickly—a couple of feet a day. It can reach 20 feet (6 m) high! The plant has very sharp spines on the tips of its leaves that can be painful if touched.

The northern region of Saint Lucia is quite wild and untamed, the opposite of so many other areas of the island. Even swimming is discouraged off this side of the coast because the water is quite rough.

Coral reefs are found on the west and south sides of the island. The southwest is also home to the city of Soufriére and its famous Sulphur Springs, a popular tourist site. This area features some of the most unusual-looking scenery on the island. The bubbling puddles of water and mud, plus the steam-filled air, make many people feel as if they have somehow stepped onto the set of a science fiction movie.

A DRIVE-IN VOLCANO

A very long time ago, Soufriére was the site of a huge volcano. Approximately 40,000 years ago, however, the volcano collapsed in a massive explosion. This left the western part of the rim empty. Today that is the opening for one of the world's only drive-in volcanoes. Vehicles can drive in and park. From there, the tour is on foot. Local guides will point out almost 2 dozen bubbling cauldrons of mud scattered over the 7 acres (2 ha). Amazingly enough, these mud holes are around 340°F (171.1°C). Steam fills the air, and anyone who visits can smell the sulphur. This volcano has not erupted for more than 200 years and is considered dormant, or inactive. Despite this, experts keep a close eye on it.

THE ISLAND CITIES

There is not a great deal of room on an island the size of Saint Lucia, so the number of cities is understandably limited. The four biggest are Castries, the capital; Gros Islet; Vieux Fort; and Micoud. Smaller cities include Anse La Raye, Canaries, Choiseul, Dennery, Laborie, and Soufriére.

Not surprisingly, Castries has the largest population, with more than 65,000, or 30 percent of the island's people. It received its name from Marechal de Castries, the French governor during the late 1700s. Located on the northwest coastline, the city has been torn down and rebuilt four times throughout its history, leaving few of the oldest buildings standing.

An aerial view of Castries, Saint Lucia's most populated city. Modern buildings have been built here and the streets are always teeming with tourists visiting the exotic island.

A "jump up" is a regular occurence on Saint Lucia that attract tourists and Saint Lucians alike.

Modern buildings have taken over and at night, the lights sparkle like never-ending fireworks. During the day, Castries bustles with tourists and locals doing their shopping. On Saturdays the noise and crowd level increase as special weekend markets open up to sell local goods. If there is a cruise ship docked in the city's harbor, the city bursts with curious visitors as well.

The second-largest city on Saint Lucia is Gros Islet with just over 20,000 people. If one asks visitors their impression of the city, they are less likely to tell you about the rows of small, clapboard houses or the flowering gardens, and are more likely to talk about the unique Friday night celebration this city features. Called the "jump up," it is a regular evening party that spills out into the city streets and neighborhoods. Starting at about 9:00 P.M., every restaurant and tavern in town turns on speakers outside of their businesses. Music of all kinds, from reggae to calypso, blasts out onto the streets, and the dancing begins. Streets are closed, and vendors sell food to hot, hungry dancers. The party goes on until the wee hours of the morning and then winds down until the following weekend.

Micoud and Vieux Fort are on the eastern part of the island. They are about the same size. They are only about 9 miles (14 km) apart and are each home to more than 15,000 people. Micoud has an interesting blend of old wooden houses and concrete, modern office buildings. The entire city consists of only a few businesses, including a post office, several restaurants, and a bank. The city is known for its wine made from such ingredients as ginger, guava, and sugar cane.

Despite its small size, Vieux Fort is considered the industrial center of the island. The island's international airport is located there, along with several malls. The city also has a theater and a police station, but no actual beachfront area to lure in tourists.

The Castries airport only has one runway.

Dennery is on the central eastern coast of Saint Lucia. About 13,000 people live there. The village features a multimillion dollar fishing port. Every weekend people are invited to the area's fish fest where, for most of the day, they can eat freshly caught fish, listen to music, and dance. It is home to lines of fishing boats carved out of single tree trunks and a brand new prison called Bordelais on the southern outskirts.

A number of the smaller cities have fewer than 10,000 people in them. The smallest of all is Canaries, which has a population of fewer than 2,000 people. Here most of the homes are clustered tightly together along the coastline.

Canaries is a tiny fishing village along Saint Lucia's coast.

A CARIBBEAN CLIMATE

As expected on a tropical island, the climate on Saint Lucia is almost as beautiful as the scenery. It is humid, but a cool breeze blows, so even with high temperatures it is not uncomfortable. The northeastern trade winds blow through at certain times of the year, and there is a definite rainy season.

The average temperature is around 80°F (26°C). There is often a light breeze and an occasional rain shower. The heat climbs during June, July, and August, with temperatures approaching 90°F (32°C). As the summer ends and fall approaches, temperatures slowly begin to drop, yet still tend to remain between 70° and 80°F (21°C to 26°C). Only in December and January does it get cold enough to think about putting on a sweater as temperatures dip into the 60s (15°C degrees).

The island's rainy season begins in June and continues to the end of November. The coastlines usually receive about 51 inches (129 cm) of rain per year, but up in the mountains, the rainfall is much higher, around 150 inches (381 cm). Of course, as with other islands, Saint Lucia is at risk during hurricane season (June to November) but because of its geographical position, it is rarely hit as hard as some other islands have been. Two exceptions have occurred, one in 1980 when Hurricane Allen destroyed many structures on the island, wiped out crops, and slowed down the tourism trade, the other occurred in 1994, when tropical storm Debby hit the island and killed several people.

Saint Lucia is susceptible to hurricanes during the rainy season from June to November.

BRIGHT, BOLD, AND BOUNTIFUL

Because of moderate temperatures, plentiful rain, and fertile soil, Saint Lucia seems to explode with color all year round. Rain forests are thick with mahogany trees. They produce unusual red and black seeds that some of the Saint Lucians use for making local jewelry. There are thick bamboo groves, acres of bright green ferns, unusual and light balsa wood trees, and colorful wild fuchsia and mountain cabbage palms.

Throughout most of the island you can see row upon row of banana trees and coconut groves. The coconut palm is often referred to as "the tree of life." It grows to 80 feet (24 m) tall and produces up to 100 coconuts a year. Every single part of the coconut palm is put to use. The large leaves are used for making roofs, hats, and baskets. The trunk is used in construction, and the other fiber and husks of the coconut itself are used to stuff products like pillows and mattresses or make ropes and brooms. Of course, the milk inside the coconut is used as a drink, and the meat is eaten raw. Coconut oil is used in cooking, making soaps, and even in brake fluid.

There are countless species of trees on Saint Lucia. Besides mahogany, banana, bamboo, and coconut, there are also mango and pineapple trees, as well as African tulips and blue mahoe. Swamps full of mangrove trees hug shorelines too.

Breadfruit trees grow tall, often reaching 60 feet (18 m) and producing huge lime-green fruit that can weigh up to 5 pounds (2 kg) each. They were first brought to the area by Captain Bligh, a famous sea commander who has been at the center of historical controversy and was the main character in the book and film *Mutiny on the Bounty*. In the late 1700s he brought over more than 1,000 saplings from Hawaii. The fruit of these trees is high in carbohydrates, and is fried, baked, roasted, and boiled for a variety of local dishes.

The breadfruit tree is a useful and important source of food to Saint Lucians.

The calabash tree is the island's national tree. It produces gourd-like fruits that the local people use as water containers, bowls, and lanterns. The juice is also boiled and turned into syrup for treating coughs and colds.

Dasheen trees have elephant ear leaves, which are often eaten and are somewhat like spinach. The fruit is boiled and tastes similar to a potato. Another fruit tree, guava, is often used to make jelly. Passion fruit trees produce fruit that contain hundreds of seeds, and the fruit is used to make juice, sherbets, and ice cream.

Saint Lucia produces a great deal of the world's nutmeg, as does its neighboring island Grenada. Nutmeg grows on trees that have fruit the size of a small tomato. The outer husk splits the shell, which is dried and ground

The calabash tree is the national tree of Saint Lucia. It reaches heights of 20 to 40 feet (6 to 12 m).

to make nutmeg, while the inside red casing is dried and crushed to make mace. Other trees on the island include pawpaw and sugar apple trees.

Just as there are a lot of trees on Saint Lucia, there are also a great many flowers. The heliconia is known as the parrot's beak flower. It has large, long leaves with pointed ends. The middle is orange-red and the rest is a soft yellow-green. Tiny orchids grow here, along with poinsettia and bird of paradise.

Saint Lucia is full of colors when its many flowers bloom. The allamanda, also known as the golden trumpet or yellow bell, has trumpet shaped blossoms. The begonia is known as the bread and cheese plant because it can be eaten. Its blossoms are sometimes sprinkled on top of salads. The chenille plant, with its long red flowers that hang like tails, is referred to as the red hot cat tail.

Lobster's claw heliconia in Saint Lucia. These flowers are also an important food source for hummingbirds.

BEWARE THE TREE!

Most of the time, trees are not considered very dangerous but in the case of the manchineel, that is not true. The manchineel has a grayish bark, with bright, shiny green leaves and small greenish flowers that turn into fruit. It typically grows along coastlines and helps provide natural windbreaks that prevent beach erosion. It is found on Saint Lucia and throughout the Caribbean.

Almost every part of this tree is dangerous. Its leaves, bark, sap, and fruit are all poisonous. Contact with any of them can cause nasty blisters. In fact, in the past, the Carib Indians used the sap of this tree to poison the ends of their darts or to contaminate the water supply of their enemies. The fruit smells and tastes sweet—but it is extremely hazardous. Just a small bite can cause swelling and blistering in the mouth and throat. Amazingly enough, even standing under the tree when it is raining is risky. The water passing over the leaves and fruit will cause burns and blisters if it touches bare skin.

Most of these trees have either a warning sign on them or a big, red X on the trunk, but some signs are missed. Tourists are constantly warned to learn what the machineel looks like and beware!

WILD AND WONDERFUL

The climate and geography of Saint Lucia lends itself to countless plants, flowers, and trees. It also supports a huge variety of reptiles, fish, and birds.

A number of birds live in the rain forests and trees of Saint Lucia. A few of them are unique to this area, including the Saint Lucia oriole, a red-billed tropical bird, and the Saint Lucia black finch. A surprising number of hummingbirds also enjoy the flowers on the island. The tiny, yellow-breasted bananaquit flits about as does the Carib grackle, a glossy black bird that looks like a crow. Other winged creatures include mangrove cuckoos, tanagers, and egrets. Gliding on the coastal winds at the shoreline, you can spy the frigate bird, a long black bird with a 7 foot (2 m) wingspan and a forked tail. Other feathered beach birds include pelicans and herons. Running to safety under the sand are tiny, edible land crabs, too.

Long ago Saint Lucia was known as Hewanorra, or "there where the iguana is found." It certainly lives up to that name as it has a wide variety

THE SAINT LUCIA PARROT

The national bird of Saint Lucia is the bright, multicolored parrot, often referred to as the *jacquot*. It is only found on Saint Lucia in the central rain forest. The parrot makes a sound that is similar to the trumpet of an elephant, only quieter. While in the shadows of the rain forest, these birds blend in. But when sunlight breaks through the leaf canopy, it is clear that this bird is anything but muted. It has blue, red, yellow, green, and white feathers. In the early morning and evening, the *jacquot* searches through the treetops for a meal, which includes different kinds of fruits and seeds.

By 1975 there were as few as 100 parrots still living in the wild. The Saint Lucia Forestry Department stepped in and banned all hunting, and started an educational program about the importance of this beautiful bird. In 1979 the parrot was declared the island's national bird, and a breeding program for the birds was started. Since these measures were taken, the *jacquot's* numbers have tripled.

The fer-de-lance snake gets its name from the French, meaning spearhead.

of reptiles running about. Along with the iguana, there are a number of snakes and lizards. The Zandoli Te is a lizard unique to this area of the world. Its numbers were threatened and now it is being slowly brought back through Saint Lucia's nature reserves programs. Geckos, known locally as *maboula*, or "evil spirits" to the Saint Lucians, are common. They primarily come out at night and make a lot of chirps and clicks as they move about. There are three types on the island. One is the common house gecko, which is about 5 inches (12 cm) long. Another is the tree gecko, a 6-inch (15-cm) tree dweller that has the ability to camouflage itself. The tiny 2-inch (5.08 cm) pygmy gecko is also found here.

Legend states that the fer-de-lance snake was the first snake brought to Saint Lucia. It was placed around the perimeter of large estates to ensure that the slaves did not attempt to escape. This brownish-gray snake has a copper-red underside. Its poison can kill a person with little effort. Another snake in the area is the Tete-Chien, or boa constrictor. It is the largest snake on Saint Lucia and although it is not poisonous, it has many fine, sharp, hooklike teeth that it uses to grab prey. It then constricts and suffocates its victim. The tiny worm snake is the world's smallest at only 6 inches (15 cm) long and one-eighth inch wide. It spends most of its life underground, eating ants and termites.

Mongooses are found on the island also. They were originally brought there to help kill the rats and have thrived ever since. Other animals include the agouti, a squirrel-like animal and the *manicou*, Saint Lucia's form of an opossum. It came to the island from Dominica in 1902 and lives in trees, coming out at night to hunt.

The island's waters have three or four different species of sea turtles, including the hawksbill, leatherback, and loggerhead. The leatherback turtle is the world's largest marine turtle and is currently considered to be endangered. It is primarily found in the northeastern part of the island, near Grande Anse. It nests only once every two to three years between March and August. During this time, the female leatherback may lay eggs 2 to 6 different times, with 60 to 120 eggs each time. The eggs mature for 60 days before hatching.

A loggerhead turtle in search of food under the Saint Lucian seas.

During nesting season, it is forbidden by law to disturb the turtles or remove or damage the eggs and hatchlings. To make sure they stay safe, Saint Lucia has instituted a program that provides guided beach patrols to walk the perimeters during nesting season and ensure the turtles are not bothered. Tourists are allowed to look from a safe distance only.

Thanks to all of the ocean water surrounding the island, marine life is rich and varied. There are coral reefs, home to hundreds of different marine species including angel and parrot fish, sea anemones, sponges, and blue tang surgeonfish. There are a number of different types of coral in Saint Lucia's waters, including deadman's fingers, staghorn, brain coral, and sea fans. In addition to these, there is also a type called fire coral that causes a very nasty stinging rash if touched.

A nesting leatherback turtle digging up nests on the seashore.

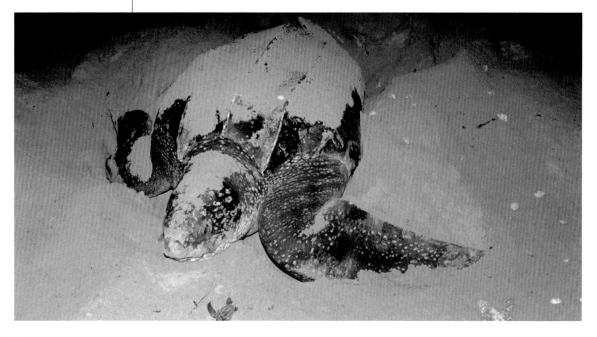

A STROLL THROUGH NATURE

One of the reasons that Saint Lucia has such a diverse and lush amount of wildlife is that the government makes maintaining and supporting nature a high priority. A number of wildlife reserves have been set up on the island. On the western side of the island is the Edmund Forest Reserve. Here tour guides take visitors through the dense rain forest. The walk is long and sometimes challenging, but also quite beautiful. Here people can see a number of transplanted species, such as the blue mahoe tree from Jamaica plus mahogany, bamboo, and mango trees. Colorful, bright flowers like African tulips, heliconia, and hibiscus make the forest bright and beautiful.

Other wildlife reserves can be found on the Maria Islands and Fregate Islands Nature Reserves in Castries, the Central Rainforest Reserve, and the Quilesse Forest Reserve. All are favorite spots for tourists and hikers.

HISTORY

SINCE THE VERY FIRST PEOPLE stepped foot on this lush island, Saint Lucia has been a coveted place. Its rich soil, thick rain forests, abundant seas, and beautiful scenery has invited many different cultures to come and stay.

The island's first inhabitants, the Ciboneys, were hunters and gatherers. Although historians know they lived on the island, little evidence remains to tell what their lives were like.

The Arawaks, an Amerindian race that most likely came from northern South America more than 1,500 years ago, followed the Ciboneys. The Arawaks were adept potters, weavers, builders, agriculturists, and shipwrights. They lived on the exterior edges of the island and survived simply by fishing, hunting, and planting crops, such as maize and cassava. Evidence shows that they liked to wear feathers and beads, and adorn themselves with tattoos. They named the island Iouanaloa.

Records suggest that the Arawaks enjoyed nearly eight centuries of peace before a new warrior group, the Kalinago, or Caribs as they were known, overpowered them. The Caribs had migrated to the area from South America. They named the island Hewanorra. The Caribs were somewhat more advanced than the Arawaks and introduced the concepts of a social system and a common language. Their tribes were ruled by kings known as caciques. They also had religious leaders called shamans. The Caribs developed a reputation for being warriors and learned how to create large war canoes. They were feared by many other islanders in the Caribbean and there were even rumors that they were cannibals.

The Caribs lived in villages that were built further inland in clearings. Huts were round, with palm thatched roofs and later, pole frames. Each cluster or settlement selected its own chieftain.

Opposite: **A canon at Fort Rodney on Rodney Bay.**

PIRATES, HO!

Little else is known about Saint Lucia's history until the turn of the 16th century. Although there is some suggestion that Columbus came across the island on his way to America in 1492, he made no official mention of it.

No one is really sure where Saint Lucia's name came from. Those who believe that Columbus came through also think that he named the island in honor of Saint Lucia, the patron saint of the Sicilian city of Syracuse.

During the 16th century, the island served as a base for pirates, as well as a hide-out for the infamous French pirate Francois Le Clerc, also known as Jambe de Bois ("Wooden Leg") because he had a wooden leg. He would wait on the island for a Spanish ship to come by and then attack it.

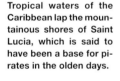

Tropical waters of the Caribbean lap the mountainous shores of Saint Lucia, which is said to have been a base for pirates in the olden days.

A GAME OF TUG OF WAR

In 1605 an English ship *The Olive Branch* was blown off course by a violent tropical storm while on its way to the South American country of Guyana. It beached on the shores of Saint Lucia. Sixty-seven people on the ship survived the tempest, but their numbers would fall quickly. They bought land and huts from the Caribs in hope of starting a new life on the island, but it was not to be. A month later, only 19 were left alive, thanks to a combination of disease and conflicts with the Caribs. The 19 survivors finally escaped in an Amerindian canoe.

Around 1600 the Dutch had set up base at the city of Vieux Fort but in 1605, England attempted to colonize the island. They failed. During the late 1630s England tried again to claim the island. Led by Captain Judlee, 300 men landed on Saint Lucia. For more than a year they lived with the Amerindians but tensions began to rise, and within three years all of the British were either dead or had fled back to England.

In 1651 the King of France claimed sovereignty over the island and gave it to the French West India Company. The Caribs were not happy about any of this and kept trying to expel the French.

Beginning in 1659 the British and French began a real tug of war over this little island. It changed hands again and again. During this tussle, most of the Caribs either ended up being killed or leaving for other islands. In 1667 the island was taken away from England and given to France through the Treaty of Breda. This treaty was signed in the Dutch city of Breda by England, the Netherlands, France, and Denmark. It arranged how different territories would be divided among those countries following the Second Anglo-Dutch War. For the next ten years, Saint Lucia belonged to the French once again. It was governed by Francis Lord Willoughby, an English baron, who was also the ruler of the neighboring islands of Barbados, Saint Vincent, and Dominica. In 1674 Saint Lucia was annexed to France and established as a dependency of Martinique, another Caribbean island between the Caribbean Sea and the North Atlantic Ocean.

England had not given up yet though. In 1686 they once again set a ship loaded with guns to take over the island and claim it as theirs. Once again they failed. The battle continued to rage on for almost another century. In 1722 England wanted to claim the island as its own, but the French refused. Finally a formal treaty was formed between the two countries. Called the Treaty of Choc, it stated that the French were to leave Saint Lucia, as well as the British, and the island was to be declared neutral until the two countries could come to better terms. Although these terms were spelled out on paper, the people chose to ignore them. They had been building homes and were not willing to walk away from them. In 1748 the Treaty of Aix La Chapelle once again stated that Saint Lucia was to remain neutral, but the claims for the land needed to be more carefully examined. Despite this, France remained in control. In 1762 England tried one more time to occupy Saint Lucia and briefly succeeded. Less than a year later, however, the Treaty of Paris, which was signed at the end of the French and Indian War, gave Saint Lucia back to the French.

France continued to develop the island. By the late 1700s a dozen towns had been founded. Sugar and cotton plantations began popping up and were thriving under slave labor. In 1778 France lost Saint Lucia one more time in the Battle of the Cul de Sac, also known as the Battle of Saint Lucia. This was a battle fought on the waters near the island between the British Royal Navy and the French Navy. Five years later, France won Saint Lucia back through the Treaty of Versailles, which also ended the American Revolutionary War.

The French Revolution (1789–99) had a significant effect on Saint Lucia. This was a period in which France worked hard to overthrow the monarchy that had ruled their country for so long. In the end, the country became an empire under the control of Napoleon Bonaparte.

This revolution resulted in the abolition of slavery in 1794. The words *Liberté, Egalité, Fraternité* (freedom, equality, and brotherhood) could be heard throughout the West Indies. The British, who were still fighting for control of the island, did not agree with the French's willingness to accept the end of slavery. Over the years, many slaves in Saint Lucia had been rushing secretly into the surrounding forests to escape the seemingly never-ending battle between France and England. These men and women came to be called *nègre marron*, although the British preferred to call them brigands, or runaways. These people survived by raiding plantations and stealing what they needed. They also tried to recruit many of the plantation slaves to join them.

The British declared war on the French living in Saint Lucia in an attempt to re-institute slavery. A man named Victor Hugues, the French Republican leader, sent his representative, Goyrand, to see if members of the *nègre marron* would fight against the British. Soon these runaways were turned into a powerful army, known as L'Armee Francaise Dans

Once a strategic point during the struggles for control of Saint Lucia between the French and British, Pigeon Island is now a national landmark and a famous tourist spot.

le Bois or The French Army in the Forest. French officers trained these new soldiers, and they fought side by side.

Hugues helped to smuggle weapons and ammunition into Saint Lucia from Guadeloupe. In the deepest darkness of the night, canoes full of the *nègre marron* silently carried the contraband across the water from ships to hidden caves on the beach. Whenever one of their canoes was found by the British, it was destroyed.

Following a victory over the British at the Battle of Rabot at Soufriére, the French Republication Army turned their eyes to the north. The only places left to attack were the fort on Pigeon Island and Fort Charlotte on Morne Fortune. When the *nègre marron* arrived, however, they were shocked to find nothing but frightened women and children there. The British soldiers had escaped to Martinique. Showing a sense of integrity and kindness, the *nègre marron* took these people onto their boats and returned them to their worried families.

Just after the turn of the 19th century, the island was once more returned to France. It stayed that way until 1814 when, in what had become a worn out pattern, it was given back to England. African slaves were brought in to help work on the growing number of sugar plantations. When slavery was abolished about 20 years later, it was a huge blow to plantation owners. They had depended on over 13,000 slaves to do the hard work they needed done in order to plant and harvest their sugar cane.

Although gaining their freedom certainly seemed like the best thing possible, for many former slaves, things got worse. Most were forced to serve a four year apprenticeship for their former owners. This meant they worked for free for at least three-quarters of the week. When the apprenticeships ended, plantation owners could no longer afford labor. The sugar cane industry began to decline and never quite recovered.

GOING FORWARD

Now that the game of tug of war seemed to be at an end, England worked hard to develop Saint Lucia. Shipping vessels were the main way to send and receive supplies and trade with other areas, and a growing number of them were steamships that ran on coal. In order to make it from port to port, coaling stations had to be established. One of these stations was on Saint Lucia. It sold enormous amounts of coal to passing ships.

As time passed, Saint Lucia gained a reputation as a harbor. By the late 1800s Castries was an important port in the world in terms of how much cargo it handled. Changes lay ahead, however. With the discovery of oil, the demand for coal began to drop quickly. In 1935 coal workers in Saint Lucia went on strike. They wanted more money. In response, the governor brought in not only a warship but marines who patrolled the streets in order to show just who was in charge. No wage increases were allowed.

THE SMALL AXE

George F. L. Charles (1916–2004) was a man whose name still commands respect throughout Saint Lucia, even after his death. When Charles died, the prime minister of Saint Lucia, Dr. Kenny D. Anthony, called him "the Father of Decolonialisaton." In his tribute at Charles's funeral, he said, "We should remember him as that rare man unchanged by power; for he remained without pomp or guile and needed no ceremony. Even as St. Lucia's first Chief Minister, he did not put on any emperor's clothes, for he possessed a moral authority which was his only garb."

George Charles helped the Saint Lucians get the right to vote for the government of their choice. He was the first chief minister. He led the first political party. He was often referred to as either Ti Jesi, Little Jesus, or Ti Hache, the Small Axe.

Charles' influence on the people was clear by who attended his funeral. As the prime minister said, "People of all walks of life turned out to pay their last respects to him. They saluted him on the Market Steps and they paid tribute to him in the house of assembly. People of all walks of life attended his funeral: laborers, clerks, public servants, merchants, government and opposition supporters, trade unionists, workers—and supporters of both the UWP and the SLP. They came to see him off because, as Monsignor Anthony said at his State Funeral service, he was among the great men of Caribbean history who made his contribution to the development of our region."

Charles was also a founding member of the Saint Lucia Labour Party (SLP). Once it was formed, the political climate of the island began to change dramatically. In 1964 the United Workers Party (UWP) won elections and by 1967, Saint Lucia had full self-government. In 1979 it gained full independence.

Two years later, the sugar workers organized their own strike. They were given a slight raise. This increased drive for better working conditions and wages resulted in the increased strength of union leaders. The Saint Lucia Workers Cooperative Union was led by George F. L. Charles, who died in 2004.

MODERN TIMES

Recent years have brought rough weather and its ramifications to the island. Hurricane Allen hit Saint Lucia in 1980. Tropical storm Debby occurred in 1994. In 2002 tropical storm Lilli destroyed a great deal of the island's banana crops, completely wiping out entire plantations in some spots.

Today Saint Lucia continues to grow and thrive, combining its new independence with island beauty and a continuing invitation for people of the world to come and explore it.

FIELDS FULL OF SUGAR

Throughout the 18th, 19th, and 20th centuries, sugar cane was the main crop found on plantations throughout the Caribbean. The only way to maintain these crops and ensure a harvest was through the use of African slaves. For years, sugar was the main crop—if not the only one—grown on the Caribbean islands.

Sugar cane is a stout, fibrous stalk that looks quite similar to bamboo. It grows between 6.5 to 19.5 feet (2 to 6 m) tall. The sugar, or sucrose, is found inside the stalk as sap. When the water in the sap is evaporated, sugar is the result. Typically the crop is harvested by hand. Before that can be done, however, the field is actually set on fire. The flames spread rapidly, burning up the dry leaves, as well as getting rid of any lethal snakes that might be living in the field. The sugar cane's stalks and roots are not hurt by the brief fire.

Next, slaves come through with special knives called machetes and cut the came just above where it comes out of the ground. A skilled worker can cut about 1,100 pounds (500 kg) of sugar cane in an hour!

After being harvested, the sugar cane is typically taken to a mill for washing, chopping, and shredding. Eventually it will be purified for cooking and other uses. In some countries, people eat the raw sugar cane cylinders to extract the sweet juice inside. Others use the juice for making a drink or adding it to the process of rum production.

GOVERNMENT

IT IS HARD TO IMAGINE that this faraway distant island in the middle of the Caribbean is independent yet still under the overall rule of England's Queen Elizabeth II, but it is. Over its history, Saint Lucia rarely had the opportunity to form a stable government simply because it changed hands so often. In 1924 it was granted representative government.

GAINING INDEPENDENCE

In 1951 Saint Lucia made a first step toward independence by granting universal suffrage, or the right to vote, to anyone over the age of 21. Briefly, from 1958 to 1962, Saint Lucia was a member of the short-lived West Indies Federation, a group of Caribbean colonies that wanted to

Left: **Great Britain's Queen Elizabeth II is the Head of State of Saint Lucia. However, the island's Governor-General acts as a Ceremonial Head of State and represents the Queen at proceedings.**

Opposite: **The parliament building on Saint Lucia.**

THE NATIONAL ANTHEM (BY REVEREND CHARLES JESSE)

Sons and daughters of Saint Lucia
Love the Land that gave us birth
Land of beaches, hills and valleys.
Fairest isle of all the earth.
Wheresoever you may roam,
Love, oh Love, our island home.
Gone the time when nations battled
For this Helen of the West!
Gone the days when strife and discord,
Dimmed her children's toil and rest.
Dawns at last a brighter day,
Stretches out a glad new way.

May the Good Lord Bless our Island;
Guard her sons from woe and harm.
May our people, live united
Strong in soul and strong in arm.
Justice, Truth and Charity,
Our ideals forever be.

Whenever the anthem is played, everyone stands at attention, men with bared heads. Commonly it is played whenever a person from the government arrives at or leaves an event and at the beginning of all public performances in a cinema or other public building.

become independent from Britain. However, the federation collapsed due to a variety of internal conflicts. In 1967, under the West Indies Act, the island became fully self-governing and responsible for itself, although the United Kingdom was still accountable for its defense. The first Saint Lucian governor was appointed. Finally, in 1979, Saint Lucia became fully independent, although still part of the British Commonwealth.

INSIDE GOVERNMENT

Saint Lucia operates under a system known as a parliamentary democracy. The queen is represented by a governor-general that she personally chooses. The governor-general's job is primarily ceremonial, although it holds on to a few powers. This position involves attending events of national importance; receiving foreign diplomatic personnel; providing leadership in Saint Lucia's social, cultural, intellectual, and economic life; and coordinating a variety of special projects.

In Saint Lucia the governor-general is a woman named Her Excellency Dame Pearlette Louisy. She was born in Laborie and has attended multiple universities. She has many degrees and specializes in education. Louisy was serving as the dean of the division of arts, science, and general studies at Sir Arthur Lewis Community College in Castries when she was chosen to be governor-general in 1997. She continues to foster her interests in the performing arts through active involvement with the island's theater and choral groups.

The residence of the governor-general's home in Castries.

The primary political power in Saint Lucia is through the position of prime minister. The current prime minister is Sir John George Melvin Compton. Born in 1926, he is more than familiar with politics and this job. He served as the island's chief minister from 1964 until 1967 and as premier from 1967 to 1979. Compton was prime minister in 1979 and then again from 1982 through 1996. He then retired but many people did not want him to and urged him to return to leadership. Even though he is now 82 years old, he believes his age is not an issue. "Age is not a factor here," he states. "I am not here running for the Olympics. Age is really a state of mind, I am giving my experience and my intelligence that God gave to me. I am not going for a marathon." As the prime minister, it is his job to oversee the rest of the government, make the most important decisions, and monitor the senate and house of assembly.

The Senate has 11 appointed members, while the House of Assembly has 17 who are elected. Six senators are appointed by the governor-general on the advice of the prime minister. Three are appointed based on the advice from the leader of the opposition. They each serve for five-year terms.

Former prime minister Kenny Anthony reminded Saint Lucians that the position of prime minister is not all-powerful as so many seem to think it is. Instead, power is spread out between the island's three main branches of government: the executive, the legislature, and the judiciary. "I pledge that this government will be a government of all the people of St. Lucia," stated Compton on the day he was sworn into office. He clearly sees a great future for Saint Lucia, especially with the World Cricket Cup taking place there. However, he also envisions a lot of changes to be made.

Saint Lucia's former prime minister, Kenny Anthony (*left*), who left office in 2006 meets with Nelson Mandela.

"For a few short weeks, St. Lucia will be on centre stage of the world," he stated in his New Year's Address to the Nation. "How we perform then will have lasting effects on our country. . . . This event can either by a "great party" . . . or one which can provide lasting benefits for both our country and our people."

The executive branch is made up of the prime minister and the Cabinet of Ministers. The legislative branch consists of all of the elected members of Parliament and the senators appointed by the prime minister, the leader of the opposition, and the governor-general. The judiciary branch is made up of the court system, the magistrate's courts, and the Supreme Court. The Supreme Court is broken into the high court and the court of appeal.

The Cabinet of Ministers in Saint Lucia is made up of a dozen ministers and two parliamentary secretaries. The ministers cover many different elements within the government including:

- Finance, International Financial Services, Economic Affairs and Information
- Education, Human Resource Development, Youth and Sports
- Commerce, Tourism, Investment and Consumer Affairs
- Communications, Works, Transport and Public Utilities
- Health, Human Services, Family Affairs, and Gender Relations
- Agriculture, Forestry, and Fisheries
- Physical Development, Environment, and Housing
- Labor Relations, Public Service, and Cooperatives
- Social Transformation, Culture, and Local Government
- External Affairs, International Trade, and Civil Aviation
- Justice
- Home Affairs and Internal Security

Saint Lucia is divided into 11 administrative divisions: Anse-la-Raye, Castries, Choiseul, Dauphin, Dennery, Gros Islet, Laborie, Micoud, Praslin, Soufriere, and Vieux-Fort. Most towns and villages are ruled by officials who were elected by the people. These local rulers perform a variety of tasks, including regulating sanitation and markets, and maintaining cemeteries and roads.

Although Saint Lucia does not have an army per se, it does have a paramilitary Special Service Unit included in its police force. It also has an active Coast Guard.

A TALE OF TWO PARTIES

There are two main political parties in Saint Lucia. The Saint Lucia Labour Party (SLP) was founded in 1950 by George F. L. Charles. It began as a trade union to support and stand up for workers' rights. The SLP won the elections in 1951 and remained in power until 1964, when the United Workers Party (UWP) was founded by John Compton. The UWP won the elections that year and again in 1982,

A NEW NATIONAL PLEDGE

In December 2003 Saint Lucia adopted the following national pledge, written by Jeff "Pelay" Elva:

With God as my guide, I pledge allegiance to my country, Saint Lucia.
I proclaim that I will serve my country with pride and dignity and will defend it with vigour and valour in the pursuit of excellence, justice and equality for all.

1987, and 1992. Compton acted as prime minister during those years until 1996, when he resigned. Dr. Vaughan Lewis then became prime minister until the following year's elections. In 1997 the SLP won all but one of the 17 seats in the Assembly in a landslide election. Dr. Kenneth Anthony was then made the island's prime minister. In the 2001 election, the SLP won again against UWP leader Dr. Morella Joseph, although with a smaller majority than before.

THE FLAG OF SAINT LUCIA

Saint Lucian artist Dunstan St. Omer designed the island's national flag. The background of the flag is a bright sky blue, often referred to as cerulean. The blue represents fidelity, or loyalty. It also stands for the island's clear blue sky and the blue of the surrounding Caribbean Sea and Atlantic Ocean.

The gold triangle stands for the unending sunshine in the region, as well as prosperity. The black and white represent the two races living on the island and working in unity.

The reason for the multiple triangular shapes is an indirect reference to the island's famous twin pitons in Soufriere. They are meant to signify hope and inspiration for the people.

ECONOMY

WITH SO MUCH RICH, fertile soil and varied plant life, Saint Lucia has supported its economy for years through agriculture. Life on such a small island makes job diversity a rarity; there simply is not enough room for hundreds to thousands of different companies as there is in larger countries of the world. For centuries, the island has had to depend on the plentiful products the people could harvest from the soil, but today that entire picture is changing rapidly.

When the Arawak and Carib people first came to the island of Saint Lucia, they turned to farming as a way to stay alive. For a brief period of time, piracy was one of the biggest money makers on the island. After the Europeans began to settle there, they developed large sugar cane and tobacco plantations. After emancipation in 1833 or 1834, however, things changed. Slavery was abolished, and free help was no longer an option.

Left: **Selling farm produce such as bananas, is still a main source of income for many Saint Lucians.**

Opposite: **Many Saint Lucian men and women work in banana plantations all over the island. Banana has become the major export product of Saint Lucia.**

By the mid-20th century, sugar cane plantations were virtually gone. In the late 1800s Castries became a major coaling station. In 1863 the first steamship docked in the capital city and filled up its boilers with coal. Within a few years, hundreds of these ships were stopping by Saint Lucia to re-fuel. That lasted until the early 1900s but was ultimately ruined by the opening of the Panama Canal, which gave ships a different route other than through the Caribbean. In addition, the Depression hit the United States, slowing down all travel and shipping. Finally coal mining disappeared almost completely after oil was discovered and production began.

GREEN GOLD

The one product that has sustained Saint Lucia's economy for almost 100 years has been what the locals refer to as "green gold," or bananas. The first attempt to grow mass quantities of the fruit was in 1925 when the Swift Banana Company bought land on the island and planted banana trees. It was a good plan, but unfortunately, it fell apart not long after when the crops were destroyed by the Panama disease, a disease caused by a fungus that attacks the roots of banana plants. It is resistant to any kind of fungicide, and cannot be chemically controlled. The company disappeared.

Seven years later, the Canadian Buying Company offered a five-year contract to the Saint Lucians. They offered to take all of the bananas the people could deliver to the wharf in good condition. The contract was a solid one, but it too fell apart a few years later when the dreaded Panama disease returned.

Foreign revenue from banana exportation has contributed greatly to the development of Saint Lucia since the 1960s. However, the banana trade has declined dramatically over the years due to competition from lower-cost Latin American banana producers.

BUNCHES AND HANDS OF BANANAS

There are three types of bananas grown on Saint Lucia. There are the typical yellow ones like those sold in most grocery stores. These originally came from Malaysia and have a sweet taste. The second type is the plantain, which is a slightly longer, harder, and darker banana. It first came from India and, unlike the usual banana, it is not eaten raw but fried or boiled and added to dishes. It has a starchy flavor similar to a baked potato. The third type is called a red banana. It is much smaller. The peel is a deep red or purple and the inside fruit is either a creamy white or slight pink. Like a yellow banana, it is eaten raw.

A new crop of bananas takes about 10 months to reach full ripeness. At first, bananas are just a cluster of flowers that grow into a group of 10 to 20 individual bananas. This group is known as a "hand."

Bananas need a great deal of care and attention. Being a banana farmer is a hard job that does not pay nearly as much as it once did.

Banana factory workers make sure that their product is of high quality for export.

When a Canadian fruit company known as Antilles Products Limited arrived in 1948, they offered Saint Lucia a 15-year contract. A Banana Grower's Association slowly formed, first with the island's largest banana producers and then including the middle and small scale farmers as well. During the 1950s the sugar industry faded away, and banana production became even more important. In addition, disease-resistant plants were developed resulting in more reliable and profitable crops.

Other companies began to take an interest in Saint Lucia's banana production and by 1957 bananas had become its chief export crop. Oddly enough, as many bananas as they produced, most Saint Lucians did not like to eat them and rarely included them in their diet.

The island joined the Windward Island Banana Trade along with neighboring islands of Saint Vincent, Dominica, and Grenada. By 1960

Saint Lucia was producing $3.5 million worth of bananas. Over the next two decades, business increased, only suffering setbacks due to an occasional drought or a passing tropical storm or hurricane. At its peak, the banana trade was supplying approximately $750,000 directly into the economy every week. The money made from this "green gold" filtered into education, construction, and the development of other crops.

DECLINING BANANA TRADE

Up until the early 1990s, the bananas that were shipped to England were given preference since Saint Lucia is part of the British Commonwealth. This special treatment had been in place since 1975, but in 1993 the European Union began restricting it and imposing a variety of tariffs and quotas that Saint Lucia had to meet. To make matters worse, the U.S. banana company, Chiquita, went to the World Trade Organization and complained about this preferential treatment. It did not take long for this news to reach Saint Lucian banana growers, and they were frightened.

Suddenly the prices that these farmers were used to earning for generations were drastically reduced; farmers did not like it. They began to strike, asking for higher returns. Things even turned violent when some farmers blocked roads and argued with police. Two farmers were killed during one confrontation. Life as a banana farmer has not been the same since.

Hundreds of farmers left the business entirely and the number of farmers and production amounts have plummeted. Sadly the many young farmers who are now unemployed have turned to the only other quick cash commodity they know of—selling drugs.

A speech by the prime minister addressed the problem of drugs on his island. He said, "Every drug trafficker is a potential enemy. Their sole purpose is to make killer drugs available to our children, our brothers, our sisters and all who will pay. They are in it only for the money, and the power. They will fry brains simply to make the money to keep their dirty and evil trade alive. . . . Drugs mean death. A life on drugs is a life wasted. We have lost too many. Now is the time to step up the fight, beginning at home."

With both a sea and an ocean on all sides, Saint Lucians have continued to fish. Most of the coastlines have multiple fishing villages scattered along them and there are entire communities that rely on what is captured from the water every day to make enough money to put food on their own tables. In 2000 almost more than 1,800 tons of fish were caught in Saint Lucia, ranging from tuna, dolphin, and snapper to kingfish, flying fish, and crayfish.

Surrounded by the sea, Saint Lucians are expert fishermen.

TOURISM IN SAINT LUCIA

As the banana trade has declined, Saint Lucians have looked quickly for other ways to keep the economy going. They have continued to grow and export other crops, including cassava and coconuts.

In the end the answer to the economical problem was found in the beauty that surrounded the Saint Lucians every day—the island itself. The rich emerald green of the trees, the deep blue of the ocean, the golden sand on the beaches, and the bright explosions of color from the rain forests were commonplace to Saint Lucians but to people in other parts of the world, it was paradise. Entertaining, hosting, and feeding these visitors became the new money maker. Tourism was the answer.

Many Saint Lucians are now working in the tourism industry.

The exotic beauty of Saint Lucia has made it become one of the most sought after wedding destinations in the world today.

Tourism took off in amazing ways. In 2005 more than 700,000 tourists visited Saint Lucia. More than half of all the people who climb on a cruise ship today will stop somewhere in the Caribbean. Of course, having more than half a million people coming to the island each year for honeymoons, cruise ship vacations, and just to see what it is like requires a lot of work but creates a lot of jobs. Many of the hotels and restaurants in Saint Lucia had to renovate and modernize. Construction took off. In 1964 there were 20 hotel rooms on the whole island. By 2000 there were almost 1,000 additional hotel rooms under construction.

Hotel managers were trained. Street vendors set up stalls on sidewalks. Parking lots were paved. Roads were improved. Maintaining natural sites like the rain forest, waterfalls, and coral reefs became a much higher priority as the government realized that by doing so, not only were they preserving their heritage but also giving tourists additional reasons to visit the island and spend money. The hard work has paid off. In 2002 the island hosted the World Travel Awards and for several years has been considered the world's leading wedding destination. The money generated from tourists makes up almost 50 percent of Saint Lucia's economy.

LEANING TOWARD DIVERSIFICATION

Saint Lucia has been diversifying beyond tourism. In recent years it has built a number of factories, including those that produce electricity, cardboard cartons, concrete blocks, clothing, rum, coconut, tobacco products, and beer. All of these provide jobs for the youth of the area.

THE PROBLEMS CONTINUE

Despite these efforts, unemployment rates in Saint Lucia remain high. There are simply not enough jobs on such a small island for all of

SIR ARTHUR LEWIS

Arthur Lewis was born in Saint Lucia in 1915. He was the fourth son of George Ferdinand and Ida Lewis. When he was 10 years old, he won a scholarship to attend the island's elite secondary school, St. Mary's. In his autobiography, he explained his rapid progress through school.

> When I was seven I had to stay home for several weeks because of some ailment, whereupon my father elected to teach me so that I should not fall behind. In fact he taught me in three months as much as the school taught in two years, so, on returning to school, I was shifted from grade 4 to grade 6. So, the rest of my school life and early working life, up to age 18, was spent with fellow students or workers two or three years older than I. This gave me a terrible sense of physical inferiority, as well as an understanding, which has remained with me ever since, that high marks are not everything.

Lewis graduated at 17 and went on to the London School of Economics. He ended up getting his Ph.D. in Industrial Economics and he was even knighted by Queen Elizabeth.

As a professional lecturer, author, and teacher, Sir Lewis helped to establish and found the Caribbean Development Bank. He wrote several books about economics and in 1979, he was awarded the Nobel Prize in Economics. He passed away in 1991 at the age of 76.

the people who live there. In addition to this, because the island is in the middle of the ocean, it has to import most of what it needs. Overall the island spends five times more on what it imports than what it earns through its annual exports.

Poverty is an issue on the island because of the high unemployment. A recent study of Saint Lucians indicated that one-quarter of the population qualified as poor, which essentially means that a family does not earn enough to cope with the daily economical demands of life. In addition, 7 percent of the population is considered indigent, or unable to feed all of its members. The study also showed that the people who lived out in the country ran twice the risk of poverty as those in the city. Many of their homes had no indoor plumbing or inadequate water supply, and some had to depend on burning kerosene for lighting.

The main causes of poverty were pointed out in the study. They included a decline in earnings from the faltering banana industry, increased competition from other places for the clothing and other products produced by Saint Lucia, and a lack of adequate education for youth in changing technology. All of this is complicated by a general lack of birth control/family planning services to prevent teen pregnancy and a lack of daycare and preschool facilities to handle these babies.

Although Saint Lucia is a vacation haven for many tourists, like any other country, looking beyond first impressions reveals underlying problems. Tourism is certainly a key element in helping the Saint Lucian economy to thrive, but it is not likely to be enough. In the coming years, Saint Lucia must also focus on developing more factories and factory jobs, encouraging people to use family planning resources, and working to improve sanitation for the poorest of its citizens.

CURRENCY AND MONEY UNITS

The monetary unit used in Saint Lucia is the East Caribbean dollar. It is used by all of the eight countries of the Eastern Caribbean Currency Union. One U.S. dollar equals $2.7 in EC. The EC dollar has been used since 1965. Before that the region used British Caribbean notes and coins.

East Caribbean coins come in the denominations of 1, 2, 5, 10, and 25 cents. There is also a dollar coin with a carving of a huge sailing ship on it. These coins are made out of a very light aluminum alloy so they are not heavy to carry.

Paper currency comes in denominations of 5, 10, 20, 50, and 100 dollars. The bills are quite colorful. Each one features a portrait of Queen Elizabeth II on the front to indicate the ongoing historical ties to Great Britain. Each bank note also carries a stamped signature by Sir K. Dwight Venner, the governor of the East Caribbean Central Bank. All notes carry a map of the eight member countries in the currency union. Each denomination features an image of different historical landmarks within the territories. The ones that feature Saint Lucia are $50 bills which show the Pitons, and the $100 bills which feature Sir Arthur Lewis, the man who won the Nobel Prize for Economics in 1979.

ENVIRONMENT

AT FIRST GLANCE, IT IS hard to imagine that Saint Lucia has any environmental problems at all. Clear blue skies carry no hint of air pollution. Sparkling ocean waters do not indicate any water pollution. Unfortunately first impressions can be deceiving. Saint Lucia deals with a number of environmental issues, just like any other country in the world.

ENVIRONMENTAL ISSUES

Nature itself has an environmental impact on the island, of course. Hurricanes and tropical storms cause beach erosion. High waves, known locally as "groundseas," also hit the shores as a result of storms out on the North Atlantic.

Left: **The beaches of Saint Lucia suffer from natural disasters that cause erosion.**

Opposite: **The view of Petit Piton from the top of Gros Piton never fails to enthrall hikers and nature lovers.**

One of the biggest environmental problems facing Saint Lucia is desertification, or the degradation of land in dry, semidry, or somewhat humid areas, usually caused by humans. Because a great deal of land has been used for producing bananas, it has resulted in a great deal of soil loss and uncontrolled water runoff during rainstorms. One way to help improve this situation is to educate farmers on where to plant and where not to plant their crops. By putting these plants on steep slopes, the runoff and soil loss are worse. Most of these farmers feel they have no other choice about where to plant, but if the right government support and education is provided, they might have a better understanding of what else they might be able to do.

Lack of knowledge and insufficient dissemination of information leads to the continuous practice of steep slope farming among farmers in Saint Lucia. Steep slope farming contributes and even worsens soil loss and erosion.

The biggest environmental dilemma that Saint Lucia faces is that the very industry that supplies the most money and jobs, also causes the most damage. The influx of thousands of tourists to the island generates income and employment but in doing so, also threatens Saint Lucia's marine, coastal, and terrestrial ecosystems.

One of the most important issues is how liquid and solid waste and waste water are handled. According to statistics, the average tourist produces twice as much solid waste as the average Saint Lucian. Cruise ship passengers are even worse, producing up to four times more during their brief stay on the

Waste in Saint Lucia is dumped in landfills which, if not maintained properly, can leak and contaminate water supply in the island.

Even the tourism industry which contributes to the island's economy poses a threat to the environment.

island. According to a recent study by the Caribbean Policy Development Centre, 75 percent of the sewage treatment and waste water treatment plants on the island do not function properly enough to keep the environment safe. This threatens marine life living near the shore and has damaged some of the coral reefs, even killing some of them. The presence of so many tourists also hurts the reefs thanks to curious divers and heavy boat anchors being dropped where they are not supposed to be. Although the government has responded to this issue by building better plants in heavily populated tourist spots, they only did so after the damages had been done.

Solid waste, or garbage, from the tourists and cruise ship passengers is another issue. Saint Lucia uses landfills to get rid of all their garbage. Recycling, composting, or burning are rarely ever done. Landfills tend to leak and contaminate water supplies, especially when overloaded by seasonal visits from tourists. Littering also causes its own problems, from plastics getting into the ocean and hurting marine animals to broken glass bottles on the beach that can potentially cause harm to someone's foot.

Clean water supplies are also a problem. The average Saint Lucian uses about 50 gallons of water per day. The average tourist uses 2 to 3 times that much. The islanders depend on surface water for their clean water supply.

BUILDING MORE AND MORE

The sights and sounds of construction are familiar in Saint Lucia, as it struggles to build hotels, restaurants, and resorts to meet the demands of the tourist trade. This has resulted in the destruction of mangroves and beaches, and has caused water pollution from sand mining, dredging, and sewage dumping. What many people failed to realize as they tore down one area for a resort is that in nature, typically one ecological region is dependent on another and another, like a line of dominos. If one region is damaged or ruined, the effects can ripple out in unexpected directions.

For example, if a mangrove swamp is mowed down in order to build another marina, the flow of freshwater changes immediately, which in turn, causes an imbalance in the makeup of the water. What was needed to allow coral reefs and fish species to survive and thrive has changed. Even the amount of sand is reduced because it is made up of the erosion of the coral and now the coral is being destroyed. This situation has happened already in Saint Lucia's Rodney Bay Marina, where a mangrove area was cut down during construction.

Fringe mangrove, also known as red mangrove at Marigot Bay.

The source of much of Saint Lucia's environmental problems lies in both the lack of adequate planning and the realization of how making one change can result in other, unexpected changes. When the Pigeon Island causeway was built, for example, it changed the flow of coastal waters so much that the near-shore fishing industry in the city of Gros Islet was almost completely wiped out.

Another area that tourism has affected in Saint Lucia is congestion on the sand, or beach overcrowding. Too many people as well as an occasional recreational vehicle on the sand make it compact tightly and this can negatively impact turtle nesting sites. Turtle hatchlings are further threatened by all of the lights along the beach and coastlines. They tend to move toward them instead of out into the ocean where they need to go to survive.

The clearing of mangrove at Rodney Bay marina has had negative repercussions on the ecosystem in that area.

A LITTLE GOOD NEWS

On the positive side, tourism has resulted in some necessary changes to Saint Lucia's environment. As more people come to see the island's many natural sites, the government has worked harder to sustain them. In recent years Saint Lucia has developed a number of environmental committees to keep a closer eye on possible problems and solutions. Money from tourist-related activities is continually allocated to funds focusing on the protection of natural resources. As Saint Lucia continues to recognize the treasures it has, it will work harder to protect them; when thousands of tourists come to the island to see its treasures, those things will still be there.

ANTI-LITTER MARCHES

In October 2006 two antilitter school marches were held in Castries and Soufriére. Directed by the Saint Lucia Solid Waste Management Authority, they were set up to help school children understand the importance of a clean environment. Each student was given a sign to carry through public areas, encouraging people to put trash were it belongs and not just throw it on the ground. Information and Education Manager Emlyn Jean said, "The marches mark the beginning of clean-up activities—an attempt to get students involved in activities where they encourage others to keep their communities clean. This year, for the first time," she continued, "we actually went to two communities." More than two dozen schools participated in the march, all rallying around the motto of "For health, for preservation, let's clean up the nation."

PIGEON ISLAND CAUSEWAY

The Pigeon Island Causeway links the 44-acre (15-ha) island to the mainland. The connection was built in 1972 so that natives and tourists could easily go to this national landmark. Although it is small, Pigeon Island features ruins of military buildings used during the battles between the French and the British for control of Saint Lucia. There is an interpretive center, which informs visitors about the rich history of the island, and a beautiful lookout point at the top of one of the forts, which gives anyone a panoramic view of the island's northwest coastline. For tourists looking for relaxation along with history, there are also two beaches and several restaurants.

People are drawn to Pigeon Island for the sites but also because it was once the hideout spot of the legendary Jambe de Bois, as well as other pirates. Its unusual history does not end there, however. Later it was a key factor in the ongoing French-British battles and just after the turn of the 20th century, it became a whaling station. In the late 1930s it was leased to an English actress named Josset Agnes Hutchinson. She left the island when a naval base was installed at Rodney Bay and then came back seven years later to start a successful yachting business. For the next few decades, Pigeon Island gained quite a reputation as a wild place to party. Hutchinson left the island to return to England in 1976, and ownership returned to Saint Lucia. In 1979 it was established as a national park.

SAINT LUCIANS

THE PEOPLE OF SAINT LUCIA all came from somewhere else. There are no indigenous Saint Lucians. The Amerindians that once lived there long ago eventually disappeared, due to a combination of disease, war, and colonization.

Today's population in Saint Lucia is a colorful and exciting mix of descendants from the many different races that came to the island as it developed. Africans, descendants from slaves brought over to take on the labor of sugar and tobacco plantations, make up about 90 percent of an estimated 168,458 people. Another group is the East Indians. They make up approximately 3 percent of the population. Their ancestors came to Saint Lucia as indentured workers once the Emancipation Act had passed and slavery had been abolished. Just about 1 percent

Left: **Saint Lucians on the streets of Castries.**

Opposite: **Saint Lucians are descendants of mixed races and cultures.**

of the population is European. They are the offspring of some of the original settlers, plantation owners, and poor laborers.

LIVING ON SAINT LUCIA

More than 30 percent of the people on Saint Lucia live in the capital city of Castries. About half of the population lives in cities. There is a definite class structure on the island. In recent years a middle class has developed, but most people fall into the rich or poor divisions, and there is a great deal of differences between them. The higher classes

Houses in the town of Soufriére.

are found in the cities, usually Castries, while the poor are more often found in the country, struggling to cope with the burdens of poverty and lack of adequate food and clean water.

Housing in Saint Lucia varies greatly depending on location and income. In the big cities and tourist areas, beautiful hotels, restaurants, and office buildings line the streets. Forty years ago much of the island was covered in graceful, tropical homes that had many windows and fancy trim. Most of these are gone now, replaced with cinder block houses that are hot, heavy, and prone to collapse under the hurricane season's high winds. Most family homes are quite small, especially in the more poverty-stricken areas of the island. As time has

As in any other country in the world, housing in Saint Lucia depends on the location and the income of a household.

marched on, the times spent out on porches and stoops have been replaced with going inside to watch television. Backyard grills and outdoor latrines have been replaced with kitchen appliances and indoor bathrooms.

There are more young people than old in Saint Lucia. Less than 10 percent of the population are over the age of 65; while more than half are under 35, and more than one-quarter are below 15. Life expectancy here is high, with men reaching an average of 70 years, while women tend to live longer to 78 years.

FOR MEN OR WOMEN

For many years, the men were in charge of Saint Lucian society. Although that is still somewhat true, the role of women has been changing with time. Men and women work side by side in the banana fields and other areas. While fishing is still a traditionally male activity, women do most of the professional cleaning and are in the majority in many of the island's factories.

As the years have passed, the women of Saint Lucia have played a more dominant role. In the home, the woman is almost always considered the head of the house. In fact, there are quite a few homes that do

not have any men in them at all. Whether it is just a mother and her children or three generations under one roof, men tend to come and go. This trend will most likely continue as more women are hired outside of the home.

GETTING MARRIED

Marriage for the Saint Lucians commonly does not happen until later in life. Instead of young people getting married, people are often middle aged. For those in the lower class, before getting officially and legally married, however, they may instead live together. The middle classes rarely do this as they tend to think it is not a respectable choice. It is not unusual for husbands to have one or more relationships with other unmarried women, but wives are not given the same opportunity.

Above: **A large family residing in Soufriére. When the parents of the family have to leave their home in search of work other family members, such as grandparents, step in to help.**

Opposite: **A woman attending to her work at a banana factory in Saint Lucia.**

Primary school students in their school uniform. Education is of utmost imporatnce to every Saint Lucian family.

Because Saint Lucians often have to move around from one place to another on the island in search of work, it is not unusual for grandparents to raise their grandchildren instead of the parents. Children living in small villages or out in the country have a great deal of freedom. They spend their days exploring the island without much adult supervision until they turn 5 and then it is time for them to start attending school.

TIME FOR SCHOOL

At the age of 5, children are sent to infant school, a type of preschool. At 8, they move onto primary or elementary school. Education is compulsory to age 15. While there are secondary schools available for older students, there are not enough places in them for all who would like to attend. Enrollment is based on the scores on their entrance exams. In 2005 approximately 60 percent of secondary school age students were able to attend school.

For many families in Saint Lucia, education is of vital importance. Families often go without many things they need in order to save the money for school books and uniforms. Overall, girls have scored higher on examinations than boys in all levels of school and women have a higher literary rate than men (90.6 percent compared to 89.5 percent).

In a speech to the people on April 10, 2006, Prime Minister Kenneth Anthony addressed the topic of Universal Secondary Education, a program the government is trying to implement on the island. It is the goal to make sure that every single student who wants a place in school will have one. "Why is Universal Secondary Education so vital to our future?" he asked.

Without education there can be no empowerment individually or otherwise.... Secondary education is vital for other reasons. Few

GOING TO COLLEGE

Most students who go through secondary school and graduate, leave the island to go to college, or university as it is called there. Many go to the United States, Canada, or Britain, while others head to the University of the West Indies (UWI). There are no colleges on Saint Lucia.

UWI was established in 1948. It currently has three campuses; Cave Hill in Barbados, Mona in Jamaica, and Saint Augustine in Trinidad. There are more than 36,000 students enrolled among its three campuses.

The government of Saint Lucia is trying to ensure that all Saint Lucian children have the best opportunities for an education possible.

can make it to University of other tertiary institutions without a secondary education. As a developing country, at least 10 percent of our secondary school population should enjoy university education. However, as of now, only 4 percent make it to university. There can be no doubt that the attainment of Universal Secondary Education will be a monumental milestone in our development.

In the speech, Anthony went on to point out exactly how the government was going to achieve this huge goal.

At the time of the speech, four new secondary schools had been built and three more were in the process. The school being built in Gros Islet is impressive. It is being constructed on 8.32 acres (3.37 hectares) in Massade. When completed, it will have 20 classrooms, 3 science labs, a computer lab, a learning resource center, an art room, segregated sick rooms for boys and girls, a staff room, offices for the administration, and an auditorium that will fit 1,000 people. This school alone will be able to accommodate 700 students.

In addition to building these new secondary schools, a few older schools are being renovated, and current secondary schools are being expanded and upgraded. "What appeared impossible has been achieved," said Anthony. "Every parent can now be secure in the knowledge that a daughter or son will no longer have to end their educational career on the benches of a primary school. This is a signal achievement that we can and must be proud of."

FOR BOYS ONLY

Saint Lucia is also home to Saint Mary's College, a Catholic secondary school for boys between 11 and 17 years old. Founded in 1890 by a Catholic priest, it currently has more than 570 students. The graduates from this school include both of the island's Nobel Laureates, as well as former Prime Minister Sir John Compton and former ambassador to the United Nations George Odlum.

Saint Mary's focuses on information technology and in 2000, opened the first computer lab. Thanks to a large U.S. donation from Bell Labs, it has 10 new high-tech computers and 12 used ones.

LIFESTYLE

LIFE ON SAINT LUCIA means many things. It means adapting to the constant presence of outsiders who bring noise and congestion, but also income. It entails coping with certain times of the year when the weather is not only uncomfortable but even dangerous. For some, it means facing the daily challenge of poverty, while for others, it is the challenge of serving and meeting the needs of tourists. Of course, life on the island also means learning to grow most of what you need because resources and supplies are limited and costly.

Opposite: **Saint Lucian boatman getting ready to meet tourists on the island.**

Below: **A typical street in the town of Gros Islet.**

THE MARKET

One of the best places to get a sense of Caribbean culture is at the central market at Rodney Bay in Castries. The ground is covered in a blanket of food, from the ever-present green and yellow bananas to huge, heavy breadfruit and piles of freshly caught fish. Other tables are filled with homemade pepper sauces, banana ketchup, or handmade baskets. Most of the tables are shaded under brightly colored umbrellas. Tourists are often greeted at the market by official guides who, for a small tip, will negotiate the way through the tangle of vendors, pointing out foods and how they are best used. The vendors are enthusiastic and eager to sell their goods and can be rather pushy to the unprepared.

A typical scene at the Rodney Bay central market on a busy day.

DRESSING ON SAINT LUCIA

In Saint Lucia, clothes are designed to be cool and comfortable in order to cope with the heat that persists for most of the year. The national dress for women is called a jupe. It is made out of a large petticoat, or skirt made out of a tough, denimlike material. This is worn with a white shirt and a colorful scarf wound around the head. It is tied so that the scarf has a peak at the top.

Saint Lucian youngsters dressed in traditional Saint Lucian attire durng a festival.

Another type of dress is called the Wob Dwiyet. It is a long dress that goes down to the ankles and usually has a pattern of flowers on it. Petticoats are worn under the dress but instead of being hidden as most are, these are deliberately longer so they stick out. This dates back to the days after the emancipation. Men known as petticoat inspectors were positioned at church doors to make sure that the black women coming to the service were wearing cotton petticoats instead of the satin ones reserved for the European women. In order to avoid being embarrassed by having to lift their skirts, the newly freed slaves wore their slips out where they could be easily seen. Traditionally a triangular scarf known as a foulard is added and worn around the neck and shoulders, and then fastened together in front with a brooch. Other fancy and heavy jewelry are added to the costume to add to the overall effect. Headpieces are often worn as well and are usually made out of the same material as the dress itself. In the past these dresses were worn by European women for ballroom dancing and other formal gatherings. Today these special dresses are reserved for special occasions, including weddings, christenings, and first communions.

RELIGION

THERE IS VERY LITTLE RELIGIOUS diversity on Saint Lucia. More than 65 percent of the people are Roman Catholic, and every village has a Catholic church in it. While other religions are scattered throughout the island, including Seventh Day Adventists, Pentecostals, and Rastafarians, they are definitely a minority.

There are also a few locals who still believe in some elements of the old West African obeah. It is based on the belief that men and women can use spells or potions from roots and plants to help heal different ailments and injuries. This concept is left over from the time before modern medicine was available on the island.

Left: **Churches are common establishments in most communities in Saint Lucia.**

Opposite: **Interior of the Cathedral of the Immaculate Conception in Saint Lucia.**

The entrance of the largest Roman Catholic church on Saint Lucia located in Castries.

CATHOLICISM

All of the traditional Roman Catholic holidays are celebrated on Saint Lucia, including Ash Wednesday, Lent, Holy Week, Good Friday, and Easter, and All Saint's Day and All Souls Day. Roman Catholicism is based on the ideas and doctrines put forth by the Pope and the Vatican in Rome. Catholics believe that Jesus Christ was the Son of God who died for the sins of the people. They also believe in God the Father, Jesus the Son, and the Holy Ghost. By accepting Jesus, believers are told they will live eternally in heaven. Catholics believe in praying to saints and that salvation is only achieved through baptism and penance for sins committed. They also believe in purgatory, while other Christian denominations believe in either heaven or hell.

Many of the schools on the island are Catholic based. Attending church each Sunday morning is a common and important event for the majority of Saint Lucians.

SEVENTH-DAY ADVENTISTS

The second-largest religious group on Saint Lucia is the Seventh Day Adventists. They are one of the fastest-growing religions today. Seventh Day Adventists are another denomination of Christianity. They believe that the Second Coming of Christ is imminent, they worship on Saturdays instead of Sundays, and they believe their bodies are temples that should be taken care of through a healthy lifestyle. This often means staying away from certain meats, especially pork (or all meat), and abstaining from alcohol, cigarettes, and nonmedical drugs.

HOLDING A WAKE

Many Catholics practice the tradition of holding a wake when someone dies and this is also true on Saint Lucia. A proper wake begins on the evening of the person's death. At least one person from each home in the village gathers to prepare the deceased. He or she is dressed in the best clothes and then laid out for guests who attend the wake to pay their respects. Those who come are often served white rum and strong coffee throughout the event, which can last all day and into the night.

Inside the house, it is common to sing hymns, and the overall atmosphere is somber and serious. Outside the house, on the other hand, is entirely different. The tone is quite festive and party-like. Music is loud and exciting. Games are played, jokes are shared, and skits are even sometimes performed. Occasionally the wake will be repeated one week later, and a Catholic Mass is held for the deceased again, a year after his or her death.

International Freight & Shipping

5 Morgraud Street, (DAHSIS BUILDING) Castries, St. Lucia. Shipping from the USA? We offer weekly reliable service from Florida to St. Lucia. Call 459-0297 for information.

Miami Receiving Address – Caribbean Freight Systems Inc. 7011 NW 87 Ave., Miami, Florida 33166, Tel: 305-629-8445. Fax: 305-629-8446

THE VOICE

THURSDAY

18 JANUARY, 2007

Vol. 119 No. 9,419

The national newspaper of St. Lucia since 1885

$1.25

The most widely-read newspaper in the country. 79% of newspaper readership: 63,700 people read the Voice.

ECONOMIC UNION

**By:-
Robertson
S. Henry**

Robertson S. Henry)

lasting 168 minutes and 155 balls while Baugh's inning was laced with six fours and one six off 53 balls.

Occasional off-spinner Liam Sebastien was the best bowler, grabbing three for 37 while Denis George and Deighton Butler took two wickets apiece.

life

OECS Secretariat release.

OECS Heads of Government wrapped up their 44th Meeting in Antigua/Barbuda Friday January 12th with the announcement of plans to press ahead with the establishment of an economic union among OECS Member States.

OECS Chairman, Prime Minister Mr. Baldwin Spencer of Antigua and Barbuda, told a post meeting press conference, the Heads endorsed a plan to go to the OECS people with a major public awareness and discussion programme on the draft Economic Union Treaty. The consultations will encompass all segments of the OECS public, including the parliamentary opposition in each member state. OECS Heads plan to be at the forefront of the entire exercise.

The draft OECS Economic Union Treaty, which will replace the Treaty of Basseterre which established the OECS back in 1981, is being developed by a regional Task Force chaired by the Governor of the Eastern Caribbean Central Bank, Sir Dwight Venner and comprising representatives nominated by each OECS Head of Government. They have engaged the services of constitutional expert Professor A.R. Carnegie, Executive Director of the

(l-r): OECS Director General Dr. Len Ishmael; Charles Savarin representing Dominica's Prime Minister, Dr. Baldwin Spencer representing Antigua/Barbuda; Prime Minister of St. Lucia; Dr. Ralph Gonsalves of St. Vincent and the Grenadines; Osborne Fleming of Anguilla; Baldwin Spencer of Antigua/Barbuda.

the OECS Authority made up of Heads of Government and granted powers to legislate in well defined selected areas with binding effect on Member States, ii) a Regional Assembly of Parliamentarians comprising government and opposition representatives of national parliaments to act as a legislative filter, iii) a Council of Ministers and an Economic Affairs Council to be charged with preparing subsidiary legislation, and

Treaty which will allow the Regional Assembly to invite non-parliamentarians with expertise in any issue before the Assembly, to participate in the debate, having been previously accorded the full rights of the Members.

The Heads mandated the OECS Secretariat to develop a proposal to establish a Unit, patterned after the CSME Unit, to drive the process of establishing the OECS Economic Union. The Heads plan to convene a special meeting prior to their

Meeting received an update from the Prime Minister of St. Vincent and the Grenadines, Dr. Ralph Gonsalves on the progress of the merger talks between CMC and Caribbean Star. Dr. Gonsalves said the Shareorg that agreement had been reached at a government to government level on the new carriers, trading as Sri and merger by the middle of the year.

The Heads expressed their appreciation for the Government of Trinidad and Tobago for putting in place

LANGUAGE

WALK DOWN ANY STREET in Saint Lucia and the language most likely to be heard is English, thanks to years of being under English control. Upon careful listening, however, another language can be heard under the surface. This is known as Kwéyòl or Creole, a combination of French, African, and Spanish. Many Saint Lucians speak it. It was originally created by African slaves as a way to talk to their French owners. Although it has been spoken on the island for years, it was not until the 20th century that anything was actually written in Creole. While most can speak it, very few can read or write it.

Left: **It is common to see signs in English on Saint Lucia. English is the predominant language spoken on the island.**

Opposite: **Saint Lucia does not have daily newspapers. The major newspaper,** *The Voice*, **is published trice-weekly.**

LANGUAGE

Creole is officially recognized by the government of Saint Lucia as a language. In 1999 the New Testament was published in Creole, a project that took 15 years to complete. In 2002 the first Creole dictionary was published by the Ministry of Education.

While the French influence can be seen throughout the island, from the names of the cities to the names of the streets and buildings, very few people actually understand and speak the language.

A CREOLE LESSON

Learning Creole is not easy because it is such a blending of different languages. Here are some common words and phrases in Creole.

Monday	*Lendi*
Tuesday	*Madi*
Wednesday	*Mèkredi*
Thursday	*Jedi*
Friday	*Vandredi*
Saturday	*Samdi*
Sunday	*Dimanch*
Good afternoon.	*Bonn apwémidi.*
What is that?	*Kisa sa a ye?*
What's happening?	*Sa ka fet?*
No, thanks.	*Non, mesi.*

SAINT LUCIAN WRITERS

Before the 20th century, some Saint Lucians were written about but very few wrote anything themselves. Derek Walcott was one of the first. He has since been followed by authors such as Garth St. Omer and Earl G. Long. Michael Aubertin, former Director of Culture, has also written a play called *Neg Maron: Freedom Fighter*, and Jacintha Lee has created a book of local legends.

Derek Walcott, a famous Saint Lucian writer, conducts literary workshops for those interested at his home on the island.

ANOTHER NOBEL PRIZE WINNER

In 1930 poet and Nobel Prize-winner Derek Walcott was born in Castries on Saint Lucia. His father was a civil servant but also a talented watercolor artist. His mother was a teacher at a local Methodist school. He began writing poetry at a young age and published many of them in his book *Collected Poems 1948–1984*. In addition to poems, Walcott wrote novels and plays, and has published a number of other books of poems. He won the Nobel Prize for Literature in 1992. His best-known play is *Dream on Monkey Mountain*, which has been performed in the Caribbean, North America, and the United Kingdom.

Derek Walcott was one of the founding members of the Saint Lucia Arts Guild, and his twin brother, Roderick Walcott, was Saint Lucia's first Director of Culture. Walcott's most expansive work is *Omeros*, which he published in 1990. Here is one of his most well-known poems from The Arkansas Treatment (1987).

Fame

This is Fame: Sundays,
an emptiness
as in Balthus,

cobbled alleys,
sunlit, aureate,
a wall, a brown tower

at the end of a street,
a blue without bells,
like a dead canvas

set in its white
frame, and flowers:
gladioli, lame

gladioli, stone petals
in a vase. The choir's
sky-high praise

turned off. A book
of prints that turns
by itself. The ticktock

Of high heels on a side walk.
A crawling clock.
A craving for work.

THE CENTRAL LIBRARY

Saint Lucia's Central Library, located in Castries, dates back to 1888 when the idea first came to mind to provide the people of Saint Lucia with free access to books and other resources. It was not until 1924, however, under the funding of the Carnegie Trust and the Castries Town Board, that the first library was built.

Saint Lucia's Central Library, which is located in Castries.

It was not long before the idea spread to other cities on the island. Today Saint Lucia has 17 library branches scattered throughout its cities and towns. In 1948 tragedy struck the main library when fire destroyed everything in it. It took two years for the building to reopen and eight years later, it was completely rebuilt.

Children on Saint Lucia are one of many who go to libraries to borrow or read books that they might not be able to afford on their own.

Currently, Saint Lucia has three main newspapers, an online information portal, and three television channels. It has several radio stations including Radio Caribbean International, and Radio 100 FM.

In 1979 the library expanded and in 1994, it was given an entire facelift when it underwent major renovations. A floor was added to make room for a larger inventory of books and other materials. Although most of the island's libraries are small, their services are appreciated by the Saint Lucians.

TIME FOR A STORY

Folklore is still very active among Saint Lucians. Tim-Tim tales, as some are called, date back to the time of slavery. They were usually told by a narrator and were about some of the funny animal characters from African tales. Stories, riddles, and proverbs are also told about animals, including Konpe Lapin (rabbit), Konpe Makak (monkey), and Konpe Tig (tiger). The trickster spider Anansi is also a popular character in stories. Anansi appeared as a man in good times, but a spider in troubled times.

A TRICKY SPIDER

In *Anasi and the Plaintains*, a Caribbean folktale by Philip Sherlock, he writes of how the spider convinced his friend the rat to share his plantains with his hungry family. At last, he had enough for his wife, Crooky, and three children. When his family saw that he was not eating, they knew they had to share.

They all broke their plantains in two, and each one gave Anansi a half. When Crooky saw what was happening, she gave Anansi half of her plantain too. So, in the end, Anansi got more than anyone, just as usual.

ARTS

SAINT LUCIA MAY BE A SMALL island but it is bursting with fascinating and varied arts and crafts. From woodcarvers to sculptors, and painters to singers, Saint Lucians know how to make their world an even more beautiful place.

The government's interest in supporting the arts has increased since the island's independence. Local businesses often take an interest in sponsoring the artists in their city.

THE VOICE OF ARTISTS

The city markets are one of the best places to see local craftsmanship. In the city of Choiseul, for example, at the Arts and Crafts Development Centre, the people are known for producing distinctive clay pots,

Opposite: **Children in Saint Lucia performing a traditional costume dance.**

Below: **A potter working clay before shaping it into a pot.**

93

carved wooden masks, and handwoven baskets. In the La Frargue craft center in southwest Saint Lucia, there are rows of potters and woodcarvers. Other artists show off their skills in studios and small stores.

In Castries you can find the shop and art studio of wood sculptor Vincent Joseph Eudovic. He first began sculpting at a very young age and won a prize for one of his sculptures at age 12. He has passed on his craft by teaching many young artists on the island. Typically Eudovic does abstract carvings of varying geometrical patterns from a variety of woods, including teak, mahogany, and red and

The shop of local wood sculptor Vincent Joseph Eudovic.

white cedar. Each sculpture is unique because no two tree roots are the same.

Another internationally known artist from Saint Lucia is Llewellyn Xavier. Born in 1945, he left the island for many years and spent some time as a monk in Montreal. He gave away all of his worldly goods. Eventually he realized that his life was meant to be spent creating art. He married and returned to Saint Lucia. Xavier was keenly aware of the environmental damage that had occurred to his homeland while he was gone. He began using his art as a form of protest and as a campaign for change. In 1993 he created what is considered his masterpiece, "Global Council for Restoration of the Earth's Environment." He used recycled materials; antique prints of birds, animals, fish and plants, and postage stamps from all over the

Saint Lucian woodcarver Vincent Joseph Eudovic (*right*) working in his workshop.

A LEADING ARTIST

One of the most well-known artists in Saint Lucia is Dunstan Saint Omer. He was born in 1927 to a Catholic family and his faith is reflected in his art. His work has been recognized all over the world. He created the island's new national flag and his murals can be spotted in a number of churches around Saint Lucia. He specializes in painting the Holy Family, as well as portraits of famous Saint Lucians. Saint Omer's work is displayed in many public buildings throughout Castries. Recently he completed a portrait of Jesus as a black man.

world to create it. It also included signatures of world environmental leaders and conservationists. In 2004 Xavier received the Order of the British Empire medal for his contribution to art. His collections have been shown throughout the Caribbean, as well as North America and Europe.

THE SOUND OF MUSIC

One thing that the entire island is known for is the many different styles of music that can be heard from one place to the next. Folk

Folk musicians on Saint Lucia.

music pours out of one restaurant, while the next one is pumping out reggae or calypso. In the square, some local musicians might be playing local styles called cadence or zouk or striking steel drums, while vendors selling street snacks often have a radio blasting out soul or rhythm and blues from the United States.

A LITTLE FOLK

One of the most common types of music on the island is folk. A typical Saint Lucian folk band usually includes instruments like the fiddle, banjo, guitar, and *chak-chak* (a type of rattle). A small, four-stringed guitar known as a *skroud* banjo is one of the most important parts of the band.

Jwé is a type of folk music that is played at dances, parties, and funerals. It is a combination of music and a commentary on politics and daily life. It is full of puns and humor. Audiences usually clap and sing along to *jwé* music. There are special dances that go along with it too. Some are done as couples, while others called *debot* and *jwé pote* are circle dances.

Quadril music is performed so that groups can dance a very formal and choreographed dance. Instruments usually include a violin, banjo, mandolin, guitar, and the *chak-chak*. The dance itself has five separate parts, and certain steps must be followed in order for it to work.

ALL THAT JAZZ

Music is always playing somewhere in the cities of Saint Lucia, but it is never quite as loud and as popular as during the island's annual Jazz Festival. People come from all over the world to be a part of this event.

Opposite: **Playing the steel drums is common among musicians on Saint Lucia.**

Below: **World renown jazz trumpeteer Chris Botti who performed at the 2007 Jazz Festival .**

The idea for the festival began in 1991. A group of people looking to boost tourism during the slower month of May began brainstorming. Hosting a jazz festival was one possibility but it was nowhere near a certainty. Other islands in the area, including Aruba and Curacao, had already tried and failed. Some people objected because jazz was not the indigenous music of the Caribbean. Why market their island with music that was not theirs, they wondered. Despite their concerns, the Saint Lucians went ahead and held the first official Jazz Festival in May 1991. Not very many people came. The small turn out was discouraging and caused some people to doubt the feasibility of organizing such a festival.

Instead of giving up, the people began looking for ways to make the festival better. They persevered and by 1994, it was becoming a truly successful venture. The music was jazz but it was a blend of acoustical, fusion, Afro-Caribbean, southern, and rhythm and blues styles. In 1999 the concert expanded to include side attractions, often referred to as "The Fringe Activities." This includes side performances by local bands as well as vendors selling food and merchandise. The program includes an opening show, main stage performances, jazz in Derek Walcott Square, Jazz in the South (in the surrounding cities of Vieux Fort, Laborie, and Soufriere) and Fringe Activities at heritage parks and beaches. The two closing days are held entirely on Pigeon Island.

American singer John Legend performing at the Jazz Festival on Pigeon Island.

Today the Jazz Festival is still going strong and is considered one of the best in the world. It is ranked second in all Caribbean festivals and among the top-five festivals in the entire world. It has been so successful that it is sold out every year. Because of limited room and resources, the festival cannot fit many more people. Instead it has extended its run to last much longer. The 2007 Jazz festival is scheduled to last 10 full days, running from May 4 through May 13.

THE QUEEN OF CULTURE

According to Saint Lucians, the name Sesenne is synonymous with culture. To many, this woman truly embodies everything that is rich and wonderful about the island.

Born in the city of Micoud in 1913, Sesenne's real name is Marie Clepha Descartes. She grew up listening to the stories, songs, dances,

---

LA ROSE VERSUS LA MARGUERITE

Each year, to remember the island's history of the tug-of-war between France and England, two groups form. Each side has a king, queen, prince, princess, and lower titles, including chief of police. In August the group called La Rose meets weekly to sing, play instruments, and dance for people. They represent the English side and are known for being loud and enthusiastic with a lot of movement built into their music. The other group called La Marguerite, on the other hand, represents the French. They gather in October and perform on Sundays. They have a reputation for melody and discipline. At both of their performances, members sing, play instruments, and dance. La Marguerite often has a large chorus with a *chantwel*, or vocal leader, while La Rose depends more on instruments like the tambourine and a wooden trumpet known as a *baha*.

and games of Saint Lucia. She absorbed all that she learned about her cultural heritage from her parents and grandparents. By the time she was 18, the people of Micoud already knew her as Sesenne, a wonderful singer. Her parents were also well known; they were the king and queen of La Rose, an annual festival held in AuguSaint. When Sesenne's father chose his daughter to be the vocal leader for his choir during the festival, even more people had the opportunity to see how talented she was.

Sesenne's abilities did not stop at singing, however. She also was a skillful dancer and she won many dance competitions. When her brother, Welson Charlery, brought some Spanish songs to the island from Cuba, Sesenne even invented some new dance steps for them.

One day a woman named Miss Grace Augustin, owner of a large guest house in Micoud, discovered Sesenne. She asked her to come and work for her at the hotel as an entertainer. Sesenne sang with a band made up of a violin, guitar, mandolin, banjo, and *chak-chak* players. From there, Sesenne began performing at other hotels throughout the area until she ran into Harold Simmons, the man known as "The Father of Saint Lucian Culture." He began recording her songs and promoting her throughout the rest of the island.

It was not long before Sesenne's voice became recognized all over Saint Lucia. At Expo '67, held in Grenada, she was chosen to represent Saint Lucia. Although she had never left the island before, Sesenne agreed. When she returned, she carried the crown for Saint Lucia. Despite her amazing success, Sesenne did not leave the island to find recording contracts and fame. Instead she stayed on her home island and raised a family. She had nine children and worked as a baker, mother, and housewife. She got involved in teaching and sharing religion with many, and also did a great deal of community work.

For all of her hard work, dedication and talent, Sesenne has been honored in many ways. In 1972 Sesenne received the British Empire Medal and in 1984, at the Catholic Church of Mon Repos, she publicly received the title of "The Queen of Culture in Saint Lucia." In 1991 she was included in the Caribbean Broadcasting Union's Hall of Fame and three years later, she received the Saint Lucia Medal of Merit. In 2000 she was awarded the Honour of the Dame Commander of the Order of the British Empire for her contribution to folk music and community service. She also received a new home, which one day will become a national museum.

MODERN SOUNDS

In the 1940s the music of Saint Lucia began to change. Calypso had arrived! This energetic style of music often includes xylophones and steel drums. It is the characteristic music that most people think

A PRIME MINISTER TRIBUTE

P.M. Kenneth Anthony honored Sesenne in 2000 when he said, "We are not just here to recognize her melodious voice, her capacity, her love to sing, but we are here with her to allow our spirits to rise with her, to find expression in all the beauty which she has given our life, and our country. But there is something that I think we need to focus on. Sesenne's contribution is really extraordinary because she has helped each and every one of us to discover ourselves, to hold on to what has made us, to reach in the deepest recesses our souls."

of when they imagine Caribbean culture. Sadly few of the calypso artists have ever been recorded because there is a complete lack of recording studios and record producers on Saint Lucia. Other modern styles have emerged in recent years, including a unique type of jazz and reggae.

Ronald "Boo" Hinkson is one of the most well-known musical performers in Saint Lucia today. He has been writing, arranging, and

Steel drums are frequently featured in calypso.

performing music for more than 30 years. His mother taught him how to play guitar as a child and he grew up listening to all kinds of jazz.

In the 1960s Hinkson formed the group the Tru Tones. Most of the members were either his friends or brothers. They were very popular throughout the island and recorded their first album in the 1970s. They made five albums altogether and even performed at the 1979 Super Bowl XIII halftime show. Later, when the group broke up, Hinkson went solo and in 1995, released his first CD called *Alive and Well*, a combination of jazz and blues Caribbean style. He writes many of his own songs and includes other Saint Lucian musical artists on his recordings.

Hinkson is now well known throughout the Caribbean and has toured in Germany, Canada, the United Kingdom, and the United States. He continues to perform at many jazz festivals and plays an active part in helping implement folk music programs into most of the public schools in Saint Lucia.

In recent years, musical heritage and tradition has certainly gained importance in Saint Lucia. From the annual Jazz Festival, which brings in thousands of people and even more revenue, to the recently created Cultural Development Foundation, it is clear that the sound of music is alive and well on this small island.

Saint Lucians, young and old, simply love music.

LEISURE

STRANGELY ENOUGH, IN THIS COUNTRY where thousands of people vacation every year in search of leisure, the Saint Lucians themselves do not often have the chance to do the same. Many of them work very hard for the money they earn and have little time left over. For those who are wealthier, leisure is usually found in the same kinds of activities as the tourists: fun in the sun and the sand, exotic restaurants, and a huge variety of sports.

Opposite: **Locals enjoying a game of dominoes in Anse La Raye.**

Below: **Horseback riding along the island's seashores is a favorite pastime not only among Saint Lucians but among tourists too.**

COME SAILING

Ever since 1986 the Atlantic Rally for Cruisers has been a regular event off Saint Lucia's shores. The race starts in November in Las Palmas de Gran Canaria and ends in Rodney Bay. It is the largest transocean sailing event in the world. More than 200 yachts compete in this 2,700-nautical-mile rally. It takes between 12 and 24 days to complete. The positions of the yachts are reported daily so that family and friends can check up on the sailors and watch their progress on the water.

On Saint Lucia the parties start the day the first ship gets into port and continue until the last one finishes the journey. The sight of the colorful, billowing sails racing across the waves is one that few people ever forget.

Tourists flock to Saint Lucia to enjoy the scuba diving, swimming, boating, sailing, wind surfing, and deep sea fishing that the water has to offer. The warm weather also makes it easy to spend time hiking mountainsides and through rain forests or golfing at a rich, green course. Horseback riding on the beach is also a favorite choice.

GOING CRICKET BARMY

The true passion for most Saint Lucians, however, is the game of cricket. They refer to their obsession with the game as being "cricket barmy." Cricket is a team sport. A match consists of two teams, each with 11 players. Matches have been known to last from a few hours to several days. Cricket is most similar to baseball, although there are definite differences. Cricket teams bat in successive innings and try to score runs. The opposing team attempts to bring an end to the other team's innings. The team with the most runs wins.

A cricket ball is hard with a cork and string center covered in leather. It is about the same size as a baseball but the leather is much thicker. Usually it is dyed red and the stitching is white. The bats are made out of willow. One side is flat and the other is humped for

England and Kenya meet one another at a test match at the Cricket World Cup held in Saint Lucia.

England's Jo Joyce in full cricket gear in a test match in Saint Lucia.

strength. The game uses wickets and posts. Players wear padding, gloves, and helmets, as well as shoes with spikes to grip the grass. The players have different positions, including bowler, wicket-keeper, striker, and nonstriker.

Saint Lucia has produced a number of excellent cricket players over the years. These include all-rounder Mindoo Phillip, batsman and wicket keeper Ignatius Cadet, and bowler Desmond Collymore.

The nation's passion for cricket can be clearly seen in the Saint Lucia Beausejour Cricket Ground. Located in the tourist area of Rodney Bay on the island's northeast side, it was once cattle pasture. The stadium covers 22 acres and can seat more than 12,000 people. It was completed in early 2002. It is a plush arena with suites for each team that feature separate gyms, balconies, lounges, and conference rooms. Darren Sammy, one of Saint Lucia's most well-known players said, "When the Beausejour Stadium was built, it really showed how serious we were about cricket, and I think now that we have such a great stadium, more and more Saint Lucians are beginning to take even more notice."

To the excitement of all the cricket fans in Saint Lucia, a good portion of the 2007 Cricket World Cup was played on their island. The Cricket World Cup is one of the world's largest and most respected sporting events. When the first one was held in the United Kingdom in 1975, the West Indies won it. The event takes places every four years and lasts for about eight weeks. The cricket world cup commenced in several different locations. During the middle leg of the tournament,

India supporters at the cricket test match against the West Indies. Many cricket fans from other countries traveled to Saint Lucia to lend support to their teams.

it was held on Saint Lucia at the Beausejour Stadium. The stadium was expanded in order to seat about an additional 8,000 people.

Sixteen different teams competed for about 47 days. The competition was divided into 4 stages that took place across 9 different countries. Saint Lucia was awarded what is known as the Blue Package, which included 6 group stage games and a semifinal game. Experts say that

Australian fans cheering on their team at Gros Islet in a match against South Africa.

at least 2 billion people tuned in worldwide. Approximately 15,000 people came to the to the island to watch in person.

To prepare for this event, the nation had to work hard. As former Prime Minister Anthony said when he addressed the nation, "There will be challenges to overcome in transportation, security, accommodation, food supply, solid waste disposal, water supply

Part of the attraction and charm of Saint Lucia is the warmth and hospitality of its people, which only serves to boost tourism.

and environmental enhancement, to name but a few areas." He also pointed out that the opportunities from such a world event as this were immense. "Some of them are obvious," he said, "such as bed and breakfast-type accommodation; the potential for our farmers to sell significantly more produce as we seek to feed large numbers of visitors; increased business for our taxi drivers, car rental companies and minibus operators and an unprecedented volume of clientele for restaurants and entertainment providers." In his opinion, however, this was just the tip of the iceberg for Saint Lucia. "If we portray an image of Saint Lucia as a beautiful island, with a friendly, hospitable and industrious people, efficiently-run services, a clean and sustainable environment, a diversified tourism product, an investor-friendly business climate, a facilitating public service and a dynamic and pro-active private sector, then the world is our oyster—in other words, the sky is the limit."

The National Sports Policy of Saint Lucia spells out just how seriously fans take sports. In the preamble the policy states, "This

MELLO THE MASCOT

He's cute. He's curious. He's a teen. Who is he? His name is Mello and he is the official new mascot for the 2007 Cricket World Cup Competition. He is an orange raccoon-like creature wearing a blue short sleeved shirt and a white vest. Some pictures show him tossing a ball in the area while leaning on a cricket bat. His eyes sparkle, his smile is genuine, and he looks happy—just the way the mascot that is the result of extensive, worldwide research and development should be.

National Sports Policy is intended therefore to serve as a vehicle to transport our sports persons and sports administrators on a journey towards improved sporting performance and attainment locally, regionally and internationally." According to this new policy, Saint Lucia's philosophy of sports is based on the recognition of the "vital importance of sports in the holistic development of the individual, the community and the nation." It goes on to say that, "Sports are an important means of building and developing the character of the individual as well as that of the community. It builds [and] nurtures the spirit of friendly competition, it provides healthy entertainment, it exercises the body, it focuses the spirit, it creates a climate of achievement and it challenges the youth in particular to higher levels of endurance and attainment."

AN OUTSTANDING ATHLETE

One of Saint Lucia's most famous athletes is cricket player Desmond Collymore. He was born in 1956 in La Brea. In 2002 he received a Saint Lucia Medal of Merit for his achievement in sports.

Prime Minister Anthony said at the award ceremony, "So you go forth with the blessings, with the recognition of the people of Saint Lucia. I say this because I think it is important that we recognise that whatever contribution that you are recognised for today does not end here. I also want to urge you to look to the future, that whatever you have done for this country, for the people of this country, for your community must not end with the medal that is pinned on your chest. There is still work to be done; a medal should never mean a retirement."

FESTIVALS

SAINT LUCIANS ENJOY celebrations. They like dressing up in special clothes and dancing and singing along to festival music. They like parades and parties. In fact, they celebrate something new every month. In addition to the traditional Catholic holidays, there are a number of other occasions that call for celebration.

Opposite: **Saint Lucians in bright, colorful costumes in celebration of Carnival.**

Below: **School children in one of Saint Lucia's numerous parades.**

CELEBRATING THROUGHOUT THE YEAR

January begins with Asou Skwe, a giant fair that is held at Pigeon Island to welcome in the New Year. Later that same month is Calypso. A number of tents are set up and each one features calypso groups that compete with each other to see who can win the competition for the title of Calypso Monarch. The audience cheers and jeers as the different bands play.

February focuses on the island's Independence Day and Carnival. Costumes are made and parades are organized. Bands practice and

Saint Lucians in Castries dressed in their costumes, participating in the Carnival festivities.

there are crowns for the king and queen. Politicians make speeches, and everyone takes a moment to reflect on the island's rich history.

March mainly centers on the Catholic celebrations of Lent and Easter. Church services are held more often than usual, and gifts are frequently exchanged in families almost like at Christmas. These are solemn holidays, especially Good Friday when the day is spent in church and Catholics are expected to abstain from anything pleasurable. Typically, on Good Friday, *akwa* or fish cakes are served on *pain d'epices*, or thin biscuits.

As spring arrives, all eyes turn to preparing for the annual Jazz Festival. June brings the Fisherman's Feast. It begins with a church service and then boats and their sheds on the beach are officially

Fishermen and their wives pulling a boat ashore. During the Fisherman's Feast, their boats and boatsheds will be blessed.

blessed. Since fishing brings food and money to the people of Saint Lucia, this is the time when it is honored. Following the blessing, people eat a lot of fish, listen to music, and dance far into the night.

WELCOME SUMMER

The summer months are packed with many different activities. The Kids' Safari Summer attracts hundreds of local and visiting children between the ages of 5 and 18. They learn about the environment, nature, folk traditions, and history. All of the vendors at the markets

Girls attending a church service. Many Saint Lucian festivals are tied in with religion. Some festivals begin with a church service before the festivities commence.

get a chance to celebrate in August at the Market Vendors' Feast. A church service kicks things off and then a feast follows. The Central Market in Castries is often the center of the celebrating; song and dance, plus endless amounts of food are offered to locals and tourists alike. August is also the month of Fet la Woz, or the Rose Festival. The classic flower is honored with great ceremony. Kings and queens are crowned and all of the local business people and government dignitaries like the prime minister and governor-general attend.

As autumn approaches, the celebrations continue. One of the biggest festivals of the entire year is Jounen Kweyol or Creole Day. On this day, Saint Lucians figuratively join hands with all of the other Creole-speaking people of the world in honor of their common culture. Traditional Creole foods are prepared and folk stories are told. Now and then people are fined for not speaking Creole, and strolling violinists supply music for everyone.

Painting grave markers on All Souls Day is one way of paying respects to and remembering the deceased.

THE ARRIVAL OF WINTER

Fet Le Mo, or All Soul's Day, is celebrated in November when Saint Lucians take time to remember loved ones they have lost. They keep

The patron saint of music, Saint Cecilia (*left*) is honored on Saint Cecilia's Day.

a lamp burning in their homes plus clean up cemeteries by repainting tombs and placing fresh flowers or wreaths at graves. On Remembrance Day, the people who have been lost in World War I and II are honored with parades and parties. Later on in the month, Saint Cecilia's Day is celebrated to respect the patron saint of music and musicians.

December is focused on the monthlong celebration of National Day, plus Christmas. National Day centers on building pride in the Saint Lucians for their country through sporting, cultural, religious, and social activities including the Festival of Lights. During this event, people compete to make the best lantern, and entire villages and towns are decorated with lights. In the past, other events have included a festival of choirs, a festival of bands, blindfolded boxing, and even a battle to see who could be the first person to catch a greased pig.

Regardless of what time of year a person chooses to go to Saint Lucia, there is always something going on to entertain, excite, and encourage visitors to stick around or come back again!

INTERNATIONAL HOLIDAY

This special day of appreciating the Creole culture began in the 1970s. Creole-speaking countries from all over the world formed a group called "Bandzil Creole" and set October 28 as the day to honor their united heritage. This includes over 15 million people across the planet. In 1984 smaller islands like Saint Lucia and Dominica decided to create a spin-off of this holiday called Jounen Kweyol or Creole Day. It is held on the Sunday that is closest to the international celebration.

Much of the day is spent exploring and understanding the heritage of the Creole people. In one spot, there might be a demonstration of old lumberjack techniques used before the invention of the chainsaw. In another location, women work hard over steaming cauldrons of farine, a product from the cassava root. Some people play an old-fashioned version of cricket called *walaba*. Traditional Saint Lucian dishes are prepared, from green figs and salt fish to lentils and crayfish.

It is a day to dress up as well. Women wear jupes, their colorful

skirts with white shirts and red ribbons. Their headpieces, known as *tete-en l'air*, are made out of a material called madras (*above*), and satin scarves go over the shoulders.

FOOD

WHILE MANY OF THE HALF million tourists come to Saint Lucia for the scenery, the music, and the water sports, a number also come for the food. Like several of the area islands, Saint Lucian food is a wonderful mixture of African, Amerindian, French, and British influences. From the street vendors offering up roasted corn to the gourmet restaurants that feature more than a dozen types of seafood, there is something for everyone to eat on this island.

Opposite: **An island chef with an array of Saint Lucian dishes.**

Below: **A vendor at the Castries Market selling fresh coconut juice.**

FRUITS, VEGETABLES, AND PROTEIN

The food that the Saint Lucians eat on a daily basis has its roots in the days when the island was full of plantations. People eat a great deal of starches found in vegetables like yams, dasheen, plantains, sweet potatoes, and breadfruit. The amount of meat in the diet often depends on the level of income in the home. If it is eaten, it is often from sources like pork hocks, pig tails, chicken back, and salt fish or cod because they are the least expensive. Until recently, green vegetables were not eaten much at all. The island's national dish is a simple one. It is called green figs and salt fish, a combination of bananas and cod.

Saint Lucians have started including green and leafy vegetables in their diet.

Most of the starchy fruits and vegetables are boiled and then mixed with varying amounts of meat. Sauces cover most dishes. Pepper sauce is found on almost every table to add heat to any dish. Banana ketchup is another condiment that can add unusual flavor.

Various condiments and sauces add flavor to the islanders' food and dishes.

ISLAND FAVORITES

The large breadfruit found on the island's trees and scattered throughout the local markets is a very versatile food that is found in many different kinds of dishes. It can be roasted and sliced. It can be cubed and put in a salad. Cassava is similar. It is commonly used to make bread but is also used as a side dish. Sometimes fish is added to it while other times sweet cherries are added to make a dessert-like dish.

Soup is an easy meal to fix and is often served in large households. Pepperpot is one of the most common soups. It is made from any variety

The breadfruit is used in many Saint Lucian dishes.

of meats and vegetables, as well as some hot peppers and cassava juice. *Souse bouillon* is another favorite. It has beef cooked with onions, beans, potatoes, and dumplings. Pumpkin soup is another choice, as is callaloo soup, which is made from the large green leaves from the dasheen plant.

In some households, fish is quite common. Since the island is surrounded by water, it gives many people the chance to fish for their dinner or at least pick up some from the market. Snapper, mahi mahi (dolphin), tuna, crab, and conch are all popular choices. Spices to bring out the flavor of the fish usually include nutmeg, cinnamon, and ginger.

Fruit abound on the island, including mangoes, pineapples, and the breadfruit which is a favorite among Saint Lucians.

BAKED PLANTAINS

2 large green plantains
½ cup breadcrumbs
1 egg
salt
2 tablespoons peanut butter
1 onion and stalk of celery, minced
½ cup milk

Boil plantains until soft and crush them while they are still hot. Add other ingredients. Blend well. Place in a dish and bake in moderate oven for 25 minutes. Serve!

PETIT PITON

¼ lb. (113.4 g) minced meat
¼ lb. (113.4 g) mixed garlic and onions, chopped
½ cup mixed vegetables
½ cup mixed parsley and celery
1 cup cooked potatoes, diced
2 tablespoons celery salt and marjoram
1 tablespoon lime juice

Place all contents together in a saucepan and simmer until cooked. Add lime juice. Make a tall pile of the cooked mixture in the middle of the plate. Surround with cooked rice. You will have your very own Petit Piton, or little mountain on your plate!

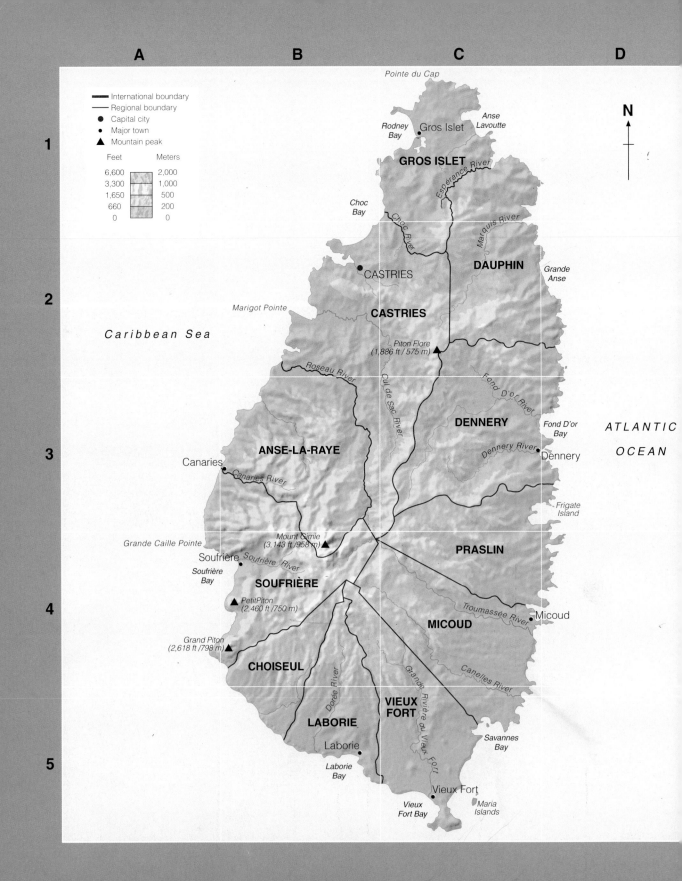

A   B   C   D

N

Pointe du Cap

Anse Lavoutte

Rodney Bay   Gros Islet

GROS ISLET

Espérance River

Choc Bay

Choc River

Marquis River

CASTRIES

DAUPHIN

Grande Anse

Marigot Pointe

CASTRIES

Caribbean Sea

Roseau River

Piton Flore (1,886 ft / 575 m) ▲

Cul de Sac River

Fond D'or River

DENNERY

Fond D'or Bay

ATLANTIC OCEAN

ANSE-LA-RAYE

Canaries

Canaries River

Dennery River   Dennery

Frigate Island

Grande Caille Pointe

Mount Gimie (3,143 ft /958 m) ▲

Soufrière

Soufrière River

PRASLIN

Soufrière Bay

SOUFRIÈRE

PetitPiton (2,460 ft /750 m) ▲

Troumassée River   Micoud

MICOUD

Grand Piton (2,618 ft /798 m) ▲

Canelles River

CHOISEUL

Dorée River

Grande Rivière du Vieux Fort

VIEUX FORT

LABORIE

Laborie

Savannes Bay

Laborie Bay

Vieux Fort Bay

Vieux Fort

Maria Islands

Legend:
— International boundary
— Regional boundary
● Capital city
• Major town
▲ Mountain peak

Feet	Meters
6,600	2,000
3,300	1,000
1,650	500
660	200
0	0

MAP OF SAINT LUCIA

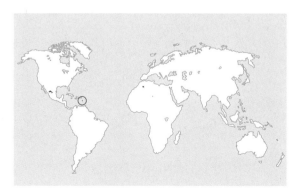

ECONOMIC SAINT LUCIA

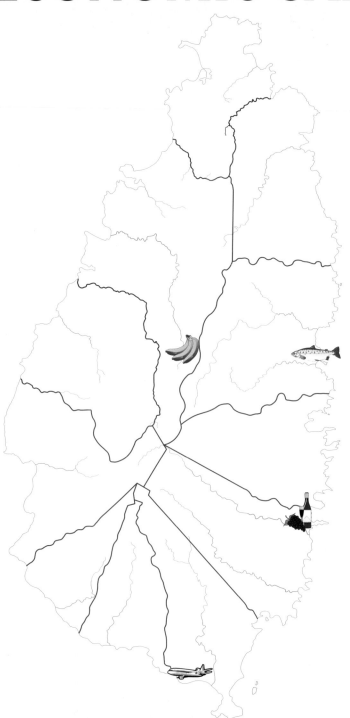

Agriculture

Banana

Manufacturing

 Wine

Services

 Airport

 Fishing port

ABOUT THE ECONOMY

OVERVIEW

Although banana production has been the mainstay of Saint Lucia's economy for the past few decades, new trade agreements and globalization are changing that picture and threatening the market. Currently the main source of income is tourism and a great deal of emphasis is being placed on maintaining that, although diversification is coming via new factories and production of other goods.

GROSS DOMESTIC PRODUCT (GDP) GROWTH RATE

$866 million

GDP BY SECTOR

Agriculture 5 percent; Industry 15 percent; Services 80 percent

ECONOMIC GROWTH

5.1 percent

CURRENCY

East Caribbean dollar (ECD)
USD1 = 2.67 ECD (2007)

AGRICULTURAL PRODUCTS

Bananas, coconuts, vegetables, citrus, root crops, cocoa

MAJOR EXPORTS

Bananas, clothing, cocoa, vegetables, fruit, coconut oil

MAJOR IMPORTS

Food, manufactured goods, machinery and transportation equipment, chemicals, fuel

MAJOR TRADING PARTNERS

United States, Trinidad and Tobago, Netherlands, Venezuela, United Kingdom, and France.

WORKFORCE

80,724

WORKFORCE BY SECTOR

Services 56.3 percent; industry 32.7 percent; agriculture 11 percent (2006 estimates)

UNEMPLOYMENT RATE

20 percent

CULTURAL SAINT LUCIA

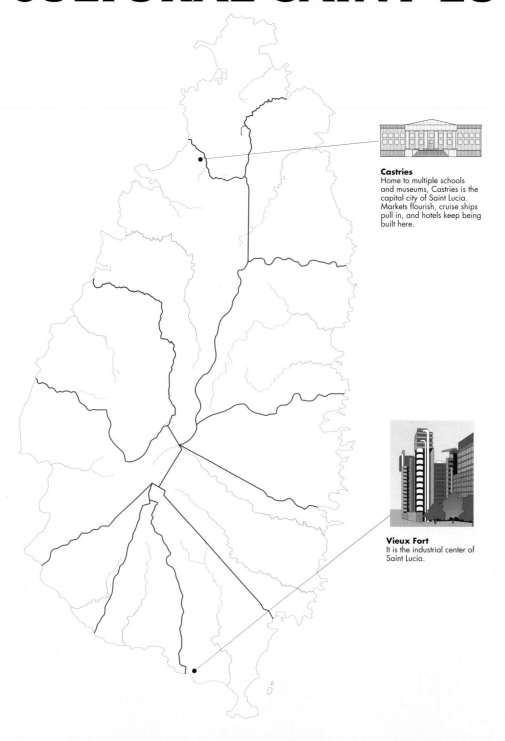

Castries
Home to multiple schools
and museums, Castries is the
capital city of Saint Lucia.
Markets flourish, cruise ships
pull in, and hotels keep being
built here.

Vieux Fort
It is the industrial center of
Saint Lucia.

ABOUT THE CULTURE

OFFICIAL NAME
Saint Lucia

CAPITAL
Castries

OTHER MAJOR CITIES
Gros Islet, Soufriére, Anse La Raye, Canaries, Vieux Fort

POPULATION
168,458 (2006 estimate)

HOLIDAYS
Independence Day (February), Good Friday/ Easter (April), Labour Day (May), Emancipation Day, Feast of Saint Rose de Lima (August), Thanksgiving Day/Feast of La Marguerite/Jounen Kweyol (October), All Saint's Day/All Soul's Day (November), Christmas (December)

ETHNIC GROUPS
Black 90 percent; mixed 6 percent; East Indian 3 percent; white 1 percent

RELIGIOUS GROUPS
Roman Catholic 67.5 percent; Seventh Day Adventist 8.5 percent; Pentecostal 5.7 percent; Anglican 2 percent; Evangelical 2 percent; other Christian 5.1 percent; Rastafarian 2.1 percent; other 1.1 percent; unspecified 1.5 percent; none 4.5 percent

LIFE EXPECTANCY
73.8 years

OFFICIAL LANGUAGE
English

LITERACY RATE
90.1 percent

LEADERS IN POLITICS
Prime Minister Sir John Compto
Deputy Prime Minister Leonard Montoute

TIME LINE

IN SAINT LUCIA	IN THE WORLD

A.D. 600
Height of Mayan civilization

1789–99
The French Revolution

1796
General Sir Ralph Abercrombie comes to Saint Lucia and takes possession following the Battle of the Saints; Castries was almost burned to the ground.

1814
Island is controlled by england again; African slaves are brought to the island to help with the plantation work.

1833 or 1834
Slavery is officially abolished.

1838
Saint Lucia is added to the new Windward Islands government.

1863
Coal mining begins.

Late 1800s
Castries is the 14th-most-important port in the world.

1914
World War I begins.

1924
Saint Lucia is granted a representative government.

1935
Coal workers go on strike for more money.

1937
Sugar workers go on strike for better conditions and money.

1939
World War II begins.

1949
The North Atlantic Treaty Organization (NATO) is formed.

1950
The Saint Lucia Labour Party (SLP) is established by George Charles.

1951
Saint Lucia is granted universal suffrage; SLP wins the election.

1957
The Russians launch Sputnik.

1958–1962
Saint Lucia is a member of the Federation of West Indies.

IN SAINT LUCIA	IN THE WORLD

1964
The United Worker's Party is formed by John Compton and wins the elections.

1966–69
The Chinese Cultural Revolution

1967
Saint Lucia has full self-government.

1972
Pigeon Causeway is built.

1979
Saint Lucia gains complete independence; Sir Arthur Lewis is awarded the Nobel Prize for Economics.

1980
Island is hit by Hurricane Allen.

1984
Saint Lucia, along with other area islands, creates the concept of Creole Day.

1986
Nuclear power disaster at Chernobyl in Ukraine

1991
First Jazz Festival is held.

1991
Breakup of the Soviet Union

1992
Derek Walcott receives the Nobel Prize for Literature.

1993
European Union begins imposing tariffs and quotas on the banana industry.

1994
Island is hit by Tropical Storm Debby.

1996
John Compton resigns and Dr. Vaughn Lewis takes over.

1997
Prime Minister Kenneth Anthony is elected for the first time.

1997
Hong Kong is returned to China.

2001
Kenneth Anthony is reelected for prime minister.

2001
Terrorists crash planes in New York, Washington, D.C., and Pennsylvania.

2002
Island is hit by Tropical Storm Lilli.

2003
War in Iraq begins.

2007
Portion of the Cricket World Cup is held in Saint Lucia.

GLOSSARY

baba
A wooden trumpet

bananaquit
A tropical bird

callalo
Dasheen leaves

debot
A circle dance

desertification
Degradation of land in dry, semi-dry or somewhat humid areas

Gros Piton
A large mountain

foulard
A silk scarf

jupe
A type of dress for daily wear

jwe
A type of Saint Lucian folk music

jwé pote
A a circle dance

kwéyol
Creole

obeah
African belief of using herbs for medicinal purposes

Petit Piton
A little mountain

Quadril
A fancy type of dance

shamans
Religious leaders

tete-en l'air
A woman's headpiece

wob dwiyet
A fancy dress for special occasions

FURTHER INFORMATION

BOOKS

Brownlie, Alison. *Landscape of St. Lucia*. London: Hodder Wayland Publishing, 2001.
———. *People of St. Lucia*. London: Hodder Wayland Publishing, 2001.
Dash, Paul. *Traditions from the Caribbean*. London: Hodder Wayland Publishing, 2002.
Feelings, Tom. *The Middle Passage: White Ships, Black Cargo*. New York: Dial Publishing, 1995.
Mohamed, Paloma. *Caribbean Mythology and Modern Life: 5 Plays for Young People*. Dover, MA: Majority Press, 2003.
Orr, Tamra. *Windward Islands*. Broomall, PA, Mason Crest Publishing, 2003.

ORGANIZATIONS

Saint Lucia Embassy
3216 New Mexico Avenue NW, Washington, DC 20016
Phone 202-364-6723

LHL Project (Lucians Helping Lucians)
C/o Keitha Glace at GlaceGrafix
18520 NW 67th Avenue, Ste. 218
Miami, FL 33015

LHL Project (Lucians Helping Lucians)
C/o Keitha Glace at GlaceGrafix
18520 NW 67th Avenue, Ste. 218
Miami, FL 33015

WEB SITES

Bulgarian National Parks. www.bulgariannationalparks.org/en/bnparks.phtml?context=category&ctg_id=25
Central Intelligence Agency World Factbook (select Bulgaria from country list). www.cia.gov/cia/publications/factbook/index.html
CIA World Factbook/Saint Lucia. www.cia.gov/cia/publications/factbook/geos/st.html
Discover Bulgaria. www.discover-bulgaria.com/
Government of Saint Lucia. www.stlucia.gov.lc/
Library of Congress Country Studies. http://lcweb2.loc.gov/frd/cs/bgtoc.html
Saint Lucia: Simply Beautiful. www.stlucia.org/
Saint Lucia Tourist Board. www.geographia.com/st-lucia/
U.S. Department of State/Saint Lucia. www.state.gov/r/pa/ei/bgn/2344.htm

BIBLIOGRAPHY

Cameron, Sarah. *St. Lucia.* Bath, United Kingdom: Footprint Handbooks, 2004.

Gordon, Lesley. *St. Lucia.* London, England: APA Publications, 2004.

Philpott, Don. *St. Lucia.* Derbyshire, England: Landmark Publishing, 2005.

"Environment and Tourism: Examining the Relationship between Tourism and the Environment in Barbados and St. Lucia" by the Caribbean Policy Development Center at www.sia-acp.org

"Poverty Assessment Report: St. Lucia" by the National Assessment Team of St. Lucia at www.caribank.org/publications/nsf/Poverty-STL?OpenPage

"Life on Tropical St. Lucia" by Kesan Gilana Clara Samuel, *New Moon Magazine,* September/October 2006, pp. 14-17.

About St. Lucia: Visual Arts. www.visitslu.com/about_slu/great_stlucians/arts.html

Adventist News Network. http://news.adventist.org

Caribbean Community Secretariat. www.caricom.org

Culture of Saint Lucia. www.everyculture.com/No-Sa/Saint-Lucia.html

Country Profile: St. Lucia. http://news.bbc.co.uk/1/hi/world/americas/country_profiles/1210491.stm

Government of Saint Lucia. www.stlucia.gov.lc

History of the Central Library of St. Lucia. www.education.gov.lc/lib/hiscentral.htm

Music of Saint Lucia. www.answer.com/topic/music-of-saint-lucia

Myhouseandgarden.com. www.myhouseandgarden.com/garden/Tropical_Plants.htm

My St. Lucia. www.mystlucia.org

Nobel Prize. http://nobelprize.org

Roman Catholic Doctrine.www.allaboutreligion.org/roman-catholic-doctrine-faq.htm

Saint Lucia National Trust. www.slunatrust.org

Saint Lucia Online. www.slucia.com

Saint Mary's College. www.bell-labs.com/user/fabian/smc/smc.htm

Sir Arthur Lewis. http://caribbean.halloffame.tripod.com/Sir_Arthur_Lewis.html

St. Lucia: City Population. www.citypopulation.de/StLucia.html

St. Lucia Jazz. http://stlucaijazz.org/jazz_articles/history.asp

St. Lucia Ministry of Agriculture, Forestry, and Fisheries. www.slumaffe.org

St. Lucia Travel Basics. www.stlucia-guide.info/travel.basics/

World Bank Notes. www.banknotes.com

United Nations Educational, Scientific, and Cultural Organization. www.unesco.org

University of the West Indies. www.uwi.edu

INDEX